Stop Bullying at Work

Stop Bullying at Work:
Strategies and Tools for HR & Legal Professionals

Teresa A. Daniel, J.D., Ph.D.

Society for Human Resource Management | Alexandria, Virginia | USA
www.shrm.org | © 2009

The Society for Human Resource Management (SHRM) is the world's largest association devoted to human resource management. Representing more than 250,000 members in over 140 countries, the Society serves the needs of HR professionals and advances the interests of the HR profession. Founded in 1948, SHRM has more than 575 affiliated chapters within the United States and subsidiary offices in China and India. Visit SHRM Online at www.shrm.org.

Interior and Cover Design: Shirley E.M. Raybuck, James McGinnis

Library of Congress Cataloging-in-Publication Data

Daniel, Teresa A., 1957-
Stop bullying at work : strategies and tools for HR and legal professionals / Teresa A. Daniel.
     p. cm.
  Includes bibliographical references and index.
  ISBN 978-1-58644-135-7
1. Bullying in the workplace. 2. Bullying in the workplace — Law and legislation. I. Title.
HF5549.5.E43D36 2009
658.3'145 — dc22

                    2009008412

Printed in the United States of America.
10 9 8 7 6 5 4 3 2 1

09-0020

Contents

Dedication

It has been said that it is only because of the work of others that we can build true knowledge. I have personally found this to be true — the prior research of the scholars and practitioners who have studied workplace bullying and other workplace incivilities was essential in helping me to make sense out of the problem as it currently exists within the American workplace.

The work of several activists and scholars — specifically, Gary and Ruth Namie, and David Yamada come to mind — significantly helped to focus public attention on the problem. Their efforts have been critical in sparking the dialogue and research that is now occurring. Without them, we would likely still be in the dark ages on this issue.

It is my hope that, collectively, our work will someday soon result in organizations where professionalism and mutual respect permeate the culture, and the problem of bullying is just a distant memory. This book is dedicated to reaching that end.

Introduction
(Or, Why Should You Care?)

II It was like Jekyll and Hyde. He was awful to everyone, literally throwing work at us. And he'd mutter about how stupid, sloppy, and incompetent we were. It got worse when the work really backed up. The added pressure put him on the edge and he really took it out on us, because he thought they'd taken away some of his clout and he needed to keep us toeing the mark. But I'll tell you, what he did had the opposite effect: He didn't respect us and we didn't give a damn about him.[1] *II*

Overview

Contrary to the expectations of most citizens, while it may be both immoral and unprofessional, it is not illegal in the United States for managers to threaten, insult, humiliate, ignore or mock employees; give employees "the evil eye"; gossip and spread rumors; withhold information that employees need to complete their work; or take credit for someone else's work. Unfortunately, these types of behaviors are not rare occurrences, but occur all too often in many American workplaces.

The physical or emotional health (and sometimes both) of employees working in organizations where these types of actions are taking place are often severely impacted. In addition, the confidence of the targeted employee is frequently so destroyed by the repeated negative actions that they lack even the courage necessary to leave such a toxic environment. Instead, they find themselves trapped in a world of psychological abuse — targets of a phenomenon that has been labeled *workplace bullying*.

The Problem of Workplace Bullying

In a nutshell, the concept of workplace bullying refers to "repeated mistreatment [against a target individual] manifested as either verbal abuse, or conduct which is threatening, humiliating, intimidating, or sabotage that interfes with work, or a combination of the three."[2] The consequences are serious, including harm to the affected individuals, their co-workers, their friends and family, as well as the organizations in which they work.

During the past decade in the United States, the issue has attracted media attention, legal attention, and union attention. Additionally, there appears to be a growing interest among academics, as well as a number of activists and research-based organizations. Internationally, the topic has received extensive attention from both academic researchers and the business community over the past 20 years. In fact, a number of countries in the European Union, Scandinavia, Australia, and Canada have actually passed legislation to protect employees from such abusive behaviors at work.

Though there were some early non-scientific or informal Internet-based polls about the incidence of bullying in workplaces across the United States, the prevalence of this issue has only recently been understood as a result of several comprehensive and in-depth scientific surveys. Three important studies released in 2007 and 2008 confirmed the seriousness of the problem in American workplaces:

- A March 2007 survey of 1,000 adults confirmed that nearly 45 percent of the respondents reported that they have worked for an abusive boss.[3]
- Similarly, a September 2007 poll found that 37 percent of American workers — an estimated 54 million employees — report being bullied at work. When organizational bystanders are included, bullying affects nearly half (49 percent) of all full- or part-time employees in America, an estimated 71.5 million workers.[4]
- In a joint study conducted by the Society for Human Resource Management (SHRM) and the Ethics Resource Center, approximately a third of HR professionals (32 percent) reported having observed misconduct that they believed violated their organizations' ethics standards, company policy, or the law. Of the top five types of misconduct witnessed, the most prevalent included "abusive or intimidating behavior toward employees (excluding sexual harassment)," with 57 percent of the participants confirming that they had witnessed this type of bullying behavior at work.[5]

Researchers in this area have compared workplace bullying to the concerns expressed about sexual harassment 20 years ago. More research is needed to generate a greater understanding of the nature and extent of the phenomenon, particularly in the United States, given that workplace bullying has been reported to be four times as prevalent as either illegal discrimination or harassment.[6]

In fact, a recent review of 100 studies conducted over 21 years comparing the consequences of an employee's experience of sexual harassment and workplace aggression found that workplace bullying appears to inflict more severe harm on employees than does sexual harassment.[7] According to the study, employees who experience bullying, incivility, or interpersonal conflict were more likely to quit their jobs, have lower well-being, be less satisfied with their jobs, and have less satisfying relations with their bosses than employees who were sexually harassed. Targets also reported more job stress, less job commitment, and higher levels of anger and anxiety.[8]

As confirmed by the recent incidence studies, the pervasiveness of the problem suggests that bullying is systemic in American business environments. As a result, this type of behavior will likely be hard to change. The degree, gravity, and regularity of workplace bullying may require law or policy changes, or both. Just as sexually harassing behavior at work was first identified as a problem and deemed unacceptable by society (and then later codified into law), workplace bullying appears to be on a similar trajectory in the United States.

Recent estimates suggest that American businesses lose approximately $300 billion per year as a result of the loss of productivity, absenteeism, turnover, and increased medical costs due to the increased stress at work.[9] In an ideal world, organizations in the United States would readily perceive the economic, operational, and morale benefits that would likely be associated with the elimination of workplace bullying. However, new workplace policies are not usually initiated by employers voluntarily; rather, they are created most often in direct response to regulatory laws and legal requirements.

The prevalence and severity of the problem and the grassroots effort to implement model legislation, coupled with the damages and costs related to the problem, suggest that companies in the United States need to elevate their attention to this issue and take the steps necessary to understand and address this workplace issue sooner rather than later.

Given that HR professionals are the corporate insiders typically charged with the responsibility for developing strategies, policies, and training to respond to new legislation or potential legal issues, this book is designed to provide not only an overview of the problem of workplace bullying, but also some practical strategies and solutions to help HR professionals and their companies proactively deal with the problem.

What Is Workplace Bullying?

*II*Homicide and other physical assaults are on a continuum that also includes domestic violence, stalking, threats, harassment, bullying, emotional abuse, intimidation, and other forms of conduct that create anxiety, fear, and a climate of distrust in the workplace. *All are part of the workplace violence problem.*[1]*II*

Descriptions of Workplace Bullies in Popular Literature

Typically, books and articles on the subject of workplace bullies in popular literature have titles that are sometimes dramatic and often inflammatory, as in these examples:

- *Brutal Bosses and their Prey,*[2]
- *Crazy Bosses,*[3]
- *Corporate Hyenas at Work,*[4]
- *Snakes in Suits,*[5] and
- *The No Asshole Rule.*[6]

Authors have referred to their books as:

- "combat guides,"[7]
- "survival guides,"[8]
- "battle tactics,"[9]
- "bully-busting strategies,"[10] or
- "a self-help book for victims"[11]

with some referring to the bully using terms such as:

- "toxic,"[12]
- "predator, sadistic, and brutal,"[13]
- "jerk,"[14] or
- "corporate psychopaths."[15]

These books variously describe and classify bullies either by the type of individual or the type of behavior most frequently used by them. Examples of a few of the most frequently cited descriptions follow:

- "Bully, Paranoid, Narcissist, Bureaucrazy, Disaster Hunter";[16]
- "Constant Critic, Two-Headed Snake, Gatekeeper, Screaming Mimi";[17]
- "Executioner, Dehumanizer, Blamer, Rationalizer, Conqueror, Performer, Manipulator";[18] and
- "Snakes in the Grass, Attilas, Heel Grinders, Egotists, Dodgers, Business Incompetents, Detail Drones, Not Respected, and Slobs."[19]

While academic critics might argue that too many books in the popular business press are often based on anecdotal evidence, all of them have contributed to the advancement of a further focus and understanding of the phenomenon of workplace bullying in the United States. In fact, many of the authors of these popular books are academics themselves; among them are Hornstein, Namie & Namie, Babiak & Hare, and Sutton. As a result, these authors are generally simply researchers who have elected to write and report on their own studies (as well as the results of others) in a style that has found a larger audience than typically occurs for academic researchers publishing in more traditional venues.

How Scholarly Literature Describes Workplace Bullies

The term "workplace bullying" has been described as a global concept that incorporates harassment, intimidation, and aggressive or sometimes violent behaviors. Several terms have been used by researchers to describe the same basic phenomenon. The term "bullying" has been used predominantly by researchers in the United Kingdom and Ireland, Australia, and Northern Europe, while German researchers have typically used the term "mobbing."

In North America, the issue has been studied under a number of different names and the research in the United States to-date is currently viewed as somewhat fragmented. Among others, these terms include:

- "workplace harassment,"
- "abusive disrespect,"
- "employee abuse,"
- "generalized workplace abuse,"
- "workplace aggression,"
- "victimization,"

- "counterproductive-deviant workplace behavior,"
- "social undermining,"
- "petty tyranny," and
- "workplace incivility."

Researchers who principally study workplace bullying and its effects have advanced several explanations of the phenomenon, but have struggled to establish a single agreed-upon definition for the problem. In fact, the existing literature reveals a relatively large number of definitions, confirming the difficulties of defining bullying.

Most of the bullying research conducted to-date has occurred predominantly in Scandinavia, the United Kingdom, Australia, New Zealand, and the European Union. While there is a growing interest in the United States about the topic, American employees remain understudied. Additionally, the experiences of American employees are potentially distinctive from those occurring in other countries, particularly in light of the "victim-blaming" that workers in the United States often direct toward the targeted individual.

Identifying and Defining Workplace Bullying

This section will review some of the most common definitions of bullying as it has been described in the United States.

One of the earliest definitions of workplace bullying was offered by Dr. Carroll Brodsky, an American psychiatrist, who defined workplace harassment (which he used as a synonym for bullying) as:

> … repeated and persistent attempts by one person to torment, wear down, frustrate, or get a reaction from another. It is treatment which persistently provokes, pressures, frightens, intimidates or otherwise discomforts another person.[20]

It has most recently been described by Drs. Gary and Ruth Namie (the two individuals considered by most to be responsible for first popularizing the term "workplace bullying" and focusing attention on the issue in the United States) as:

> … repeated, health-harming mistreatment, verbal abuse, or conduct which is threatening, humiliating, intimidating, or sabotage that interferes with work or some combination of the three.[21]

Social psychologist and professor Loraleigh Keashly referred to workplace bullying as:

> ... "emotional abuse" characterized by "hostile verbal and nonverbal, nonphysical behaviors directed at a person(s) such that the target's sense of him/herself as a competent person and worker is negatively affected.[22]

Professor Joel Neuman, a prominent researcher on workplace aggression and conflict, succinctly defined bullying as involving "deliberate, hurtful and repeated mistreatment of a target."[23]

Researchers Noa Davenport, Ruth Schwartz, and Gail Elliott emphasized the effects of abusive group behavior on the individual, adopting the term "mobbing" (which is commonly used in Europe). They described bullying as:

> an emotional assault. It begins when an individual becomes the target of disrespectful and harmful behavior. Through innuendo, rumors, and public discrediting, a hostile environment is created in which one individual gathers others to willingly, or unwillingly, participate in continuous malevolent actions to force a person out of the workplace.[24]

Legal scholar and author of model anti-bullying legislation David Yamada suggested that each of these definitions includes certain characteristics that should be included in any understanding of workplace bullying. He summarized the phenomenon as follows:

> In sum, workplace bullying can be described as the intentional infliction of a hostile work environment upon an employee by a coworker or coworkers, typically through a combination of verbal and nonverbal behaviors.[25]

Pamela Lutgen-Sandvik, an academic researcher from Arizona State University, expanded the Namies' earlier description of bullying by stating that:

> Workplace bullying, mobbing and emotional abuse — essentially synonymous phenomena — are persistent, verbal

and nonverbal aggression at work that include personal attacks, social ostracism, and a multitude of other painful messages and hostile interactions.[26]

With her colleagues Sarah Tracy and Janet Alberts, Pam Lutgen-Sandvik also described workplace bullying this way:

Numerous negative interactions that feel intimidating, insulting or exclusionary constitute bullying — actions targeted workers typically believe are intentional efforts to harm, control, or drive them from the workplace."[27]

The Workplace Bullying Institute defined the phenomenon of bullying as:

... repeated, health-harming mistreatment of one or more persons (the targets) by one or more perpetrators that takes one or more of the following forms: verbal abuse; or offensive conduct/behaviors (including nonverbal) which are threatening, humiliating, or intimidating; or work interference — sabotage — which prevents work from getting done.[28]

In the United States, this definition appears to be gaining in use. In fact, it is this definition that has also been proposed in the proposed model anti-bullying legislation discussed in Chapter 8.

Typical Actions of a Workplace Bully

Now that you have a solid working understanding of the concept of workplace bullying, we will turn our focus to the specific actions taken by a bully at work so that you can identify them more quickly.

The 2007 U.S. Workplace Bullying Survey, a collaborative project between the Workplace Bullying Institute and Zogby International researchers, included interviews with 7,740 respondents.[29] It was the largest national survey of a scientifically representative sample of adult Americans on the topic — ever. According to this research, the "negative acts" of a workplace bully (along with the percentage of respondents reporting such conduct) most typically included the following:

- Verbal abuse (shouting, swearing, name-calling, malicious sarcasm, threats to safety, etc.): 53 percent;
- Behaviors/actions (public or private that were threatening, intimidating, humiliating, hostile, offensive, inappropriately cruel conduct, etc.): 53 percent;
- Abuse of authority (underserved evaluations, denial of advancement, stealing credit, tarnished reputation, arbitrary instructions, etc.): 47 percent;
- Interference with work performance (sabotage, undermining, ensuring failure, etc.): 45 percent;
- Destruction of workplace relationships (among co-workers, bosses, or customers): 30 percent;
- Other: 5 percent;
- Not sure: 0.5 percent.

Similarly, early studies by Harvey Hornstein[30] noted "eight daily sins" of bullying bosses. These "sins" included the following negative boss behaviors:

- Deceit: lying, giving false or misleading information through acts of omission or commission;
- Constraint: restricting subordinates' activities in domains outside of work (for example, where they live, the people with whom they live, friendships, and civic activity);
- Coercion: threatening excessive or inappropriate harm for noncompliance with a boss's wishes;
- Selfishness: protecting themselves by blaming subordinates and making them the scapegoats for any problems that occur;
- Inequity: providing unequal benefit or punishment to subordinates due to favoritism or non-work related criteria;
- Cruelty: harming subordinates in normally illegitimate ways, such as public humiliation, personal attack, or name-calling;
- Disregard: behaving in ways that violate ordinary standards of politeness or fairness, as well as displaying a flagrant lack of concern for subordinates' lives; and
- Deification: implying a master-servant status in which bosses can do or say whatever they please to subordinates because they feel themselves to be superior people.

The U.S. Workplace Bullying Survey (2007) recently reported that a majority of the mistreatment that occurs is *overt*, with a majority of targets (54 percent) reporting that the bullying mistreatment occurred openly in front of others. Only 32 percent said it was conducted behind closed doors, and 10 percent said it occurred in an office with the door kept open so others could hear. Some gender differences among bullies also emerged in the study, with 57 percent of male bullies reportedly using public bullying tactics (as compared to 49 percent of female bullies) and 47 percent of female bullies conducting the mistreatment behind closed doors (compared to just 38 percent of male bullies).

Confirming the incidence of mistreatment occurring openly in front of others, in the Workplace Bullying Institute 2008 Labor Day Survey, 95 percent of the respondents indicated that they had actually witnessed the mistreatment or abuse at least once, while 97 percent said they were "aware" of the problem.[31]

Although many researchers have included physical abuse in their categorization of bullying, they all agreed that the behaviors involved in workplace bullying are mainly of a *psychological* rather than a *physical* nature. In fact, acts of actual physical violence tend to be rather rare in bullying. The key difference between the kind of "normal" conflict that occurs with some frequency in most work environments and bullying is not necessarily *what* is done and *how* it is done, but rather the *frequency* and *duration* of what is done.

As noted previously, bullying is repeated, persistent, and continuous behavior, "marked by the characteristic features of frequency, intensity, duration, and power disparity." For example, isolated occasions where a person is given a job to do that is below their level of competence, is given a tight deadline, or is not asked to join colleagues for lunch or another social event would most likely be seen as normal occurrences that are, unfortunately, just a fact of most people's work lives and would not be considered bullying. However, such actions *can* become bullying behaviors when they are used in a systematic manner over a longer period, resulting in an unpleasant and hostile work environment.

Bullying as a Process

It has been suggested that bullying may follow an escalatory pattern over time — moving from less to more severe behavior. As a result, it is not an "either-or" phenomenon, but is often a rather gradually evolving process.

During the early phases of the bullying cycle, targets are typically subjected to aggressive behavior that is difficult to identify as bullying because it is often indirect and discreet. More aggressive acts occur later in the cycle. The target is isolated and avoided, humiliated in public by excessive criticism or by being made a laughingstock. In the end, both physical and psychological means of violence may be used by the bully.

Four stages of development have been identified as typically occurring during the bullying process.[32] They are as follows:

- Aggressive behaviors — may be characterized as indirect aggression, which is often difficult to recognize because of its subtlety;
- Bullying — may be characterized by a stage of more direct negative behaviors, often leaving the target humiliated, ridiculed, and increasingly isolated;
- Stigmatization — as a result of the negative acts directed toward them, the targets become stigmatized and find it more difficult to defend themselves; and
- Severe trauma — at this point in the process, the target may suffer from a wide range of stress symptoms (for example, become withdrawn, reluctant to communicate for fear of further criticism, increase dependence on alcohol or other substances, poor concentration, etc.).

According to this process model, bullying tends to start with a situation where rather subtle but aggressive behaviors are directed against one or more persons. When the target begins to feel the effects of the bullying, the target has problems putting forth a defense. The bully often takes advantage of his or her more powerful position to intensify the aggression in an effort to ensure that the target is seen as "the problem" by the organization. As a result, the mental and physical health of the target is affected — often dramatically.

Another model[33] also suggested that bullying can be viewed as a process, suggesting five different phases that are distinguished as follows:

- Phase 1: Conflict — is characterized by a critical incident, a conflict;
- Phase 2: Aggressive Acts — is characterized by aggressive acts and psychological assaults that set the bullying dynamics in motion;
- Phase 3: Management Involvement — involves management in the negative cycle through its misjudgment of the situation. Instead of extending support, management begins to isolate and/or expel the target;

- Phase 4: "Branding" the Target — brands targets as "difficult" or "mentally ill" people. This misjudgment by management and/or health professionals (and sometimes both) serves to reinforce the negative cycle; and

- Phase 5: Expulsion — is the point at which the target actually leaves the organization, either voluntarily or by forced resignation or termination. The trauma of this event can, additionally, trigger post-traumatic stress disorder (PTSD). After the target has left the organization, the emotional distress and the ensuing psychosomatic illnesses frequently continue, and often intensify.

The process of bullying is best viewed visually (see Figure 2.1) so that you can see the interaction between the typical phases.

Figure 2.1 Bullying as a Process

Source: Leymann, 1996, p. 171.

A Systemic Perspective of Workplace Bullying: A Higher-Level View

In addition to viewing bullying as a process, it may be helpful to think about the issue of bullying from a systems-related viewpoint. This view allows you to step back from the problem to obtain a more abstract and higher-level understanding of the particular "pivot points" that create a workplace situation that enables individuals to misuse and abuse their power at work.

When considered from this perspective, HR practitioners must look at five key factors that are inextricably linked. These include the following:

- The personality of the bully (e.g., is the bully so self-interested that he or she fails to follow corporate policies, etc.?);
- The organizational culture ("how things are done around here," including management style, work environment, stress, ethics, organizational structure, etc.);
- The personality of the target (e.g., is he or she a "weak sister," poor performer, dependent, defiant, or too aggressive, etc.?);
- External factors that may impact the organization (e.g., current state of the industry, downsizings, potential mergers or acquisitions, etc.); and
- The triggering event that begins the conflict (did the organization fail to train its people about how to manage and resolve conflict, or did the company avoid the issue, even after being notified that a problem was developing?).

A visual model may help to depict how these factors interact with one another. A systems model of bullying is in Figure 2.2.

"Degrees" of Workplace Bullying

Does the severity or intensity of the hostile workplace behaviors have any bearing on whether or not the issue is identified as bullying? The short answer is *yes*. A consensus seems to have developed that these various forms of hostile behaviors arrange themselves along a continuum of increasing severity. For example, behaviors captured under the terms "emotional abuse," "psychological aggression," and "incivility" are often characterized as low-intensity or low-level bullying, while forms of physical violence (such as assault, rape, and homicide) are considered to be "extreme forms" of bullying.

As a result, it has been suggested that bullying can be identified

Figure 2.2 A System View of the Problem

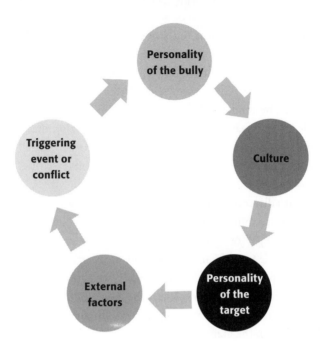

according to *degrees*, based on the different effects that bullying has on an individual.[34] Similar to the way different degrees of injury from burns are classified, bullying has been classified based on three degrees as follows:

- First-degree bullying: The individual manages to resist, escapes at an early stage, or is fully rehabilitated in the same workplace or somewhere else;
- Second-degree bullying: The individual cannot resist, nor escape immediately, and suffers temporary or prolonged mental and/or physical disability, and has difficulty re-entering the workforce; and
- Third-degree bullying: The affected person is unable to re-enter the workforce. The physical and mental injuries are so severe that rehabilitation seems unlikely.

Comparisons to Domestic Violence

It has been said that being bullied at work most closely resembles the experience of being a battered spouse.[35] The abuser (the bully) inflicts pain when and where he chooses, keeping the victim (target) off balance with the knowledge that "violence can happen on his whim but dangling the hope that safety is possible during a period of peace of unknown duration."[36]

The target is kept close to the abuser by the nature of the relationship between them (e.g., husband to wife, boss to subordinate, or co-worker to co-worker). The victim of the abuse frequently doubts himself or herself, often engaging in self-blame. The abuser exploits his or her power, real or imagined. Then witnesses, bystanders, observers, friends, and family evolve from denial to acknowledgment that the abuse is real, to rationalizing the motives of the abuser, and then blaming the victim for staying in the "toxic" relationship with little sympathy for impersonal factors that could explain the victim's apparent inaction.[37]

From a distance, it often appears too easy and even socially acceptable to denigrate bullied individuals. Disparaging comments such as "they are such whiners" or "wimps" or "babies" are all too common. Organizations often fail to stop bullying out of fear or a desire not to interfere with a situation that is viewed as a "private, interpersonal conflict" that the parties should work out between themselves. The problem is the power differential — usually the target is in an inferior organizational position without much (if any) power to do anything to stop the abuse.

History confirms that American society was slow to respond to domestic violence, preferring instead to consider the matter to be a confidential family matter. Eventually, though, domestic violence was criminalized because of its devastating impact on its mostly female victims. Private abuse thereafter became a public concern. As a result, domestic violence is no longer legal or acceptable to society. If the proposed "Healthy Workplace Bill" (see Chapter 8 for further information about the model anti-bullying legislation) is enacted, someday the same may be said for workplace bullying.

Wrap-Up

Now that you have an overview of how to understand bullies' actions and the typical process that occurs when one employee bullies another, you will be better prepared to identify those situations requiring your attention (and intervention) more quickly. Importantly, Chapter 9 will provide you with a more detailed discussion of a bully as compared to a manager simply operating as a "tough boss" so that you will be able to more easily identify the difference and respond appropriately.

The "Players" in a Bullying Situation

//Bullying is not a management style; it is abuse. It is about anger and aggressiveness.[1]//

Bullying has been described as involving a power imbalance of a "victim-perpetrator" dimension — the target is subjected to negative behavior on such a scale that he or she feels inferior in defending himself or herself in the actual situation. Importantly, it must be noted that conflicts between parties of perceived equal strength are not considered bullying.

To understand the dynamics of a bullying situation, it is essential to define the "players" in a typical workplace bullying incident. These include (a) the bully, (b) the target, (c) the "organizational bystanders," (d) other family and friends, and (e) the organization. Characteristics of each of these participants are further described as follows:

The Bully

According to the most recent scientific survey of the issue in America, the U.S. Workplace Bullying Survey (2007)[2] reported the following profile of a bully:

- 60 percent of bullies are men, while 40 percent are women;
- 73 percent of bullies are in a supervisory position;
- When the bully is a female, 71 percent of the targets are women;
- When the bully is a male, 53 percent of the targets are men;
- Bullies operate alone in 68 percent of the cases, at least in the beginning of the conflict; and
- Bullies have an "executive sponsor" in 43 percent of bullying situations (meaning an individual who is more senior to the bully who is likely to protect the bully from being disciplined for the abusive behaviors, even if the bully is publicly exposed).

Conversely, some studies have reported that *co-workers* are most often the source of workplace aggression. Surprisingly, instances of "upward bullying" have also been reported where subordinates are the aggressors toward their bosses; however, despite occurrence rates of between 2 percent and 27 percent, cases of upward bullying are reported rarely. Still, bullying behavior can exist at any level of an organization — bullies can be supervisors, subordinates, co-workers, and colleagues.

Harvey Hornstein[3] identified three prevalent types of bully personalities:

- Conquerors — bullies interested in power and control and "protecting their turf";
- Performers — bullies who suffer from low self-esteem yet belittle their targets; and
- Manipulators — bullies who are self-interested and vindictive, often taking credit for the work of others and never taking responsibility for their own mistakes.

Gary and Ruth Namie[4] also identified three types of bullies, which differed somewhat from Hornstein's classification. These included:

- Chronic Bullies — those who bully because of their personality development. They inflict harm on others, end careers, and "shatter the emotional lives of their targets" and are frequently characterized by feelings of personal inadequacy and self-loathing. In fact, targets report that "staring into the face of their bully, they swear they are looking at the devil personified."
- Opportunistic Bullies — those who choose to bully as part of their tactics to prevail in office politics and who may be able to suspend their aggressive characteristics away from work; and
- Accidental Bullies — those who are truly unaware of the effect of their actions on other people and, when confronted about their behavior, typically retreat and apologize, never making the same mistake again.

In addition, they suggested that another category of bullies may also exist and referred to this group as "Substance-Abusing Bullies," meaning those individuals who persistently abuse alcohol or drugs.

Clinical psychologist Keryl Egan[5] attempted to categorize and explain the different types of bullies by the types of behavior that they practice. Egan suggested that bullying behavior moves along a continuum, with three clearly identifiable types marking differences in bullying behaviors as follows:

1. Type 1: "The Accidental Bully" — includes "insensitive, aggressive and demanding behaviors which have as their aim some 'higher good' such as getting things done, reaching high standards, beating the competition or the financial survival of the company. Although the person behaving this way may normally relate reasonably well to others, they regard tough, insensitive and driven behavior as normal in a pressured workplace. The health and well-being of others is either not considered or is secondary to primary business goals. Such people are often shocked when they are made aware of the consequences of their attitudes and actions."

2. Type 2: Destructive, Narcissistic Bullying — includes " ... destructive, self-absorbed attitudes and behaviors [that] feature a lack of any form of empathy, blaming, nitpicking, devaluing others, lies, boasting, and taking credit for others' work. This kind of bullying, particularly if it is by a leader or manager, discourages initiative in staff and frequently is accompanied by chaotic, disorganized work processes. What may start out as simply self-absorbed behavior may become more vengeful and intentionally harming to others when under pressure."

3. Type 3: Serial Bullying — includes "the most destructive kind of bullying because it sets about systematically and subtly to subvert the health, well-being and career prospects of others. There is no concern about the organization and self-interest is paramount." Chaos and conflict frequently follow in the wake of a serial bully.

Research about the types of situations where bullying seems to originate suggests that there are two primary types of bullying which are discussed as follows:[6]

- Predatory bullying: In cases of predatory bullying, the target has personally done nothing provocative that could reasonably justify the behavior of the bully. In these types of situations, the target is accidentally in a situation where a bully is demonstrating power or is exploiting the weakness of an accidental victim. This is similar to the concept of "petty tyranny," referring to leaders who "lord their power over others through arbitrariness and self-aggrandizement, the belittling of subordinates, lack of consideration, and the use of an authoritative style of conflict management." In some organizations, bullying seems to be more or less institutionalized as part of the normal leadership and managerial practices.

■ Dispute-related bullying: Conversely, dispute-related bullying occurs as a result of highly escalated interpersonal conflicts. The difference between normal interpersonal conflicts and bullying is determined by the frequency, intensity, and duration of the behavior, as well as the ability of both parties to defend themselves in the situation.

Though far from complete, the evolving research suggests that certain patterns of workplace bullies appear to be emerging.[7] These patterns include the following:

■ Bullies are likely to be male and/or of institutionally superior status to the target;

■ Bullying behaviors vary widely, covering a variety of overt and covert and verbal and non-verbal acts that undermine a target's ability to succeed at his or her job; and

■ Bullies seek out agreeable, vulnerable, and successful co-workers, often motivated by the bullies' own feelings of inadequacy.

The Target

For purposes of this study, the individuals subjected to the bullying behavior are referred to throughout the discussion as "targets." In the U.S. Workplace Bullying Survey (2007), a number of significant findings were reported that contribute to a better understanding of the typical profile of the individuals targeted for such workplace abuse.

With respect to targets, the key findings of this survey were as follows:

■ 57 percent of those employees targeted for the bullying abuse are female;

■ Female bullies target female employees in 71 percent of the reported situations;

■ 55 percent are "rank-and-file" employees;

■ 45 percent suffer stress-related health problems (with 33 percent of the targets suffering from such problems for more than one year);

■ 40 percent of the bullied individuals never complain or report the abuse to their employers;

■ 24 percent of the targets were terminated, while 40 percent voluntarily left the organization and 13 percent transferred to another department within the same company;

- Only 4 percent complain to state or federal agencies; and
- Only 3 percent ever file a lawsuit.

While the mythology surrounding bullying is that targets complain and litigate frequently, this recent research clearly dispelled those myths. In addition, post-research found that targeted individuals suffer debilitating anxiety, panic attacks, clinical depression (39 percent), and even post-traumatic stress disorder, generally referred to as PTSD (30 percent of the women and 21 percent of the men).

It has been suggested that targets experience "causal trauma" as a result of bullying — a trauma which thereafter leads to what is referred to as "traumatizing consequential events."[8] This perspective suggests that a target's psychological problems following a bullying incident will be escalated if the bullying behaviors occur over a long period *and* are followed by a "rights violation" (such as an injury to the target caused by an unfair organizational response or a failure of the legal system to provide protection). This additional new trauma and the additional sources of anxiety often occur just at the time that the individual experiences a rights violation by his or her company that further undermines the target's self-confidence and psychological health.

Given that targets of workplace bullying reportedly endure an average of 18-20 months of exposure to the bullying actions, it is apparent that specific instances of bullying typically take place over a fairly long period of time for employees in the United States. As a result, it appears that there is a clear link between the length of exposure to the negative acts and the stress-related issues occurring as a result of the bullying that were reported by 45 percent of the participants in the U.S. Workplace Bullying Survey (2007).

There is also evidence to suggest that racial and ethnic minority employees are more likely than non-minority workers to be the targets of racial/ethnic bullying. In addition, those who experience racial/ethnic bullying are more likely to experience general bullying at work as well.

Targets have reported that they anticipate the workday with a sense of dread and impending doom — that they are not able to relax and focus on doing the job due to their constant anxiety about the next attack. Privately, targets report that they are "profoundly ashamed" of being victimized and are confused and frustrated at their apparent or perceived inability to fight back and protect themselves.[9]

In addition to their participation in "self-blame," targets are often blamed by others because such others think that the targets have somehow done something to "deserve" the mistreatment. In the U.S. Workplace Bullying Survey (2007), when asked to explain why the target was mistreated, 13 percent noted that it was due to "some aspect of the target's personality." This tendency to "blame the victim" is much like what was historically done to victims of both sexual harassment and domestic violence. Due to the persistency of these types of attributive behaviors among their colleagues in the workplace, targets often find themselves isolated, demoralized, and unable to escape or prevent the bully from continuing these terrorizing tactics.

Some targets have explained the experience like this: "I feel like I have 'kick me' tattooed on my forehead." The shock of being singled out for repeated abuse at work can be as traumatic as divorce or a loved one's death and can evoke levels of anxiety and psychological pain necessitating professional help. In fact, the process of bullying has been referred to as "psychological terror"[10] for the targeted individuals. Others have noted that the experience of being bullied can be fully comparable with PTSD from war or prison camp experiences.

One common thread in all abusive types of relationships is the element of dependency. With respect to bullying, the abuser in the situation most often controls some important resources in the target's life (for example, pay, promotions, etc.) so the targeted individual is, indeed, somewhat dependent on the abuser.

It has been theorized that targets remain in these sorts of abusive types of work relationships due to economic dependence, learned helplessness, and a fear of the unknown. The U.S. Workplace Bullying Survey (2007) confirmed this dimension of dependence in the bully-target relationship, reporting that targets "rarely confront the bully or act in an adversarial manner." Survey respondents reported the following actions taken by targets to try to solve the problem:

- 40 percent took no action;
- 38 percent complained *informally* to a superior;
- 15 percent filed a *formal* complaint with HR and/or senior management;
- 4 percent filed a *formal* discrimination complaint with a state or federal agency; and
- Only 3 percent ever filed a lawsuit in court.

Earlier studies suggested that targets may remain in an abusive situation or avoid reporting the harmful conduct for several reasons, including the fear of speaking up, fear of potential retaliation, as well as indecision about whether or not the behavior was inappropriate. In fact, retaliation for reporting mistreatment is not an unfounded fear; those who report such abuse are, in fact, often the targets of additional abuse.

These research findings challenge the expectation that people can, will, or even should self-report the problem because the targets may be vulnerable to being victimized even further after reporting the mistreatment. As a result, targets may choose silence over reporting and continue to suffer the abuse or its untreated effects.

The "Organizational Bystanders"

Within an atmosphere of fear and mistrust, other employees who witness bullying (the so-called "organizational bystanders") may experience feelings of helplessness, frustration, and a lack of control, as well as anger at the organization for not dealing with the bully's behavior. They may also spend time worrying about whether they will be the bully's next target — and with good reason: as many as 80 percent of workers say that they have witnessed bullying sometime during their career.

Researchers have also found increased symptoms of depression, anxiety, and psychosomatic complaints in those who were not the actual victims of the abuse, but who were simply witnesses present in the work environment. These organizational bystanders also reportedly experience increased fear, emotional exhaustion, hyper-vigilance, stress, and stronger intentions to leave.

Most employees understand that challenging the status quo likely involves significant risk. As a result, instead of protesting the bullying behavior, employees on the sidelines often rally in support of the bully out of fear of reprisal and self-protection. This weakens the possibility of the target forming support coalitions with fellow co-workers; however, a full 20 percent of all witnesses reportedly leave their organizations as a result of the situation.

In the most recent U.S. survey — the Workplace Bullying Institute 2008 Labor Day Survey[11] (a follow-up to the 2007 study) — when asked if any of the target's co-workers (of any rank, peers or managers) had actually witnessed the mistreatment at least once, 95 percent said "yes." When asked if the target's co-workers were aware of the mistreatment, 97 percent said "yes." But when asked what the co-workers actually *did* in response to seeing the mistreatment, the participants reported the following:

- 0.8 percent — they banded together and confronted the bully as a unit, stopping the bullying;
- 7.1 percent — they offered specific advice to the target about actions he or she should take to stop it;
- 28.4 percent — they gave only moral and social support;
- 15.7 percent — they did and said nothing, not helping either the target or the bully;
- 13.2 percent — they voluntarily distanced themselves from the target, isolating him or her;
- 4.8 percent — they followed the bully's orders to stay away from the target;
- 12.9 percent — they betrayed the target to the bully while appearing to still be friends;
- 14.7 percent — they publicly sided with the bully and acted aggressively toward the target; and
- 2.5 percent — reported that they were "not sure."

Although nearly all of the target's co-workers were aware of the mistreatment, in 46 percent of the situations, co-workers abandoned their bullied colleagues, while in 15 percent of the cases co-workers became actively aggressive toward the target, and did nothing at all in 16 percent of the cases. To be fair, co-workers did take positive action in 36 percent of the cases, but it was predominantly limited to offering moral support — anonymously and from the safety of the sidelines.

Interestingly, in less than 1 percent of all situations did a workgroup band together to confront the bully in an attempt to stop the abusive treatment of their colleague. Why? They reported that they were afraid of the bully in 55 percent of all cases.

Other Family and Friends

Bullying can also have negative (and sometimes disastrous) effects on interpersonal relationships and family functioning, frequently resulting in divorce or estrangement from the target due to the impact of the stress and other psychological trauma of the bullying. In fact, family and friends are often considered to be "co-victims" in the bullying situation.

The Organization

Though often neglected in discussions of those involved in a workplace bullying incident, organizations actually play a significant role in the process. In the U.S. Workplace Bullying Survey (2007), the study indicated that when informed about the bullying in their organization, employers took the following actions:

■ In 18 percent of the situations, the employer actually made the problem worse;

■ In 44 percent of the reported bullying incidents, the employer either escalated the problem for the target or it did nothing; and

■ In only 32 percent of the situations did the employer help or try to assist in resolving the situation.

What this survey indicated was that in a full 62 percent of all bullying situations, employers either made the problem worse or *did nothing.* This is an astonishing statistic, and one that suggests a need for HR professionals to get proactively involved in the management of this issue — and quickly.

Similar to the U.S. Workplace Bullying Survey (2007), a Workplace Bullying Institute survey asked the following question in its 2008 Labor Day Survey:

At work, have you experienced any or all of the following types of repeated mistreatment: sabotage by others that prevented work from getting done, verbal abuse, threatening conduct, intimidation, or humiliation?[12]

When the employer was notified about the bullying behavior, this study suggests a response rate as follows:

■ 1.7 percent — conducted a fair investigation and protected the target from further bullying with negative consequences for the bully;

■ 6.2 percent — conducted a fair investigation with negative consequences for the bully, but the target was retaliated against;

■ 8.7 percent — conducted an inadequate/unfair investigation with no consequences for either the bully or the target;

■ 31.0 percent — conducted an inadequate/unfair investigation with no consequences for the bully, but the target was retaliated against;

■ 12.8 percent — did nothing or ignored the complaint, with no consequences for either the bully or the target;

- 15.7 percent — did nothing, and the target was retaliated against for reporting the abuse but the bully kept his or her job; and
- 24.0 percent — did nothing, and the target was retaliated against and eventually lost his or her job.

Let's consider what these statistics really mean: these facts suggest that employers did nothing to stop the bullying in 53 percent of all reported cases, and actually retaliated against the target in 71 percent of the incidents! In 40 percent of all cases, the targets considered the employer's investigation to be inadequate or unfair, with less than 2 percent describing the employer's response as fair and safe. Filing complaints led to retaliation by employers in 24 percent of the situations (and the resulting job loss of the employee filing the complaint). And astoundingly, the bullies were disciplined in only 6.2 percent of the reported incidents.

The study's results also confirmed earlier findings that targets are not "wimps or whiners" as they are derisively dismissed sometimes. To the contrary, no formal complaint was ever filed by the target with their employer in 50.7 percent of all reported cases.

Prevalence of the Problem

*❙❙*I once worked with a guy who was really engaging and easy to talk to. He always had an ambitious streak (and he wasn't at all shy about it), but nothing that would send up any red flags. Once he achieved a position of authority, though, he seemed to take on an entirely different personality. He became a "my way or the highway" kind of guy. In meetings he would openly ridicule and humiliate his staff members, often reducing them to tears. Later they would just be so angry that they could hardly function. I don't think he ever admitted he was wrong about anything from the moment he acquired authority. When I ran into him socially after that, he could still conjure up that engaging guy I used to know, but it became increasingly difficult to ignore the impact of his work persona. It was toxic.[1]*❙❙*

Popular media regularly features stories concerning the pervasiveness of bullies in the workplace, and, as mentioned in Chapter 2, bookstores around the country stock numerous books about toxic bosses.

The AFL-CIO labor union has even gone so far as to institute an online contest that seeks to name the worst boss in the country in its *"My Bad Boss"* contest.[2] A similar site, www.ebosswatch.com, seeks to level the playing field by providing a place where employees can post the names and egregious actions of particularly abusive bosses.

At its 2007 National Conference on Professional Responsibility, the American Bar Association acknowledged the prevalence of the problem within its own professional ranks in a session titled "Law Firm Bullies: What Makes Them Tick and How to Control Them."[3] In addition, the American Psychological Association (APA) honors "Psychologically Healthy Workplaces" with an award each spring in an effort "to promote employee health and well-being, while also enhancing organizational performance."[4] The award recognizes the value of healthy workplaces and is intended to motivate companies to take steps to create a positive work environment. Given the prevalence of bullying and its negative health effect on employees, the eradication of bullying practices is among the type of negative workplace actions that the APA seeks to promote.

In an effort to provide the evidence which suggests that this issue is one worth acting on now, the following section will explore the American incidence rate of bullying.

Prevalence Rates in the United States

Though there have been a number of non-scientific or informal Internet-based polls about the incidence of bullying in U.S. workplaces, it is only recently that the issue has been confirmed through comprehensive and in-depth scientific surveys. Three important recent studies confirm the seriousness and prevalence of the problem in American workplaces.

These recent surveys include several key studies.

Employment Law Alliance Survey (2007)

A March 2007 survey[5] of U.S. adults (which surveyed 1,000 employees, and included extensive interviews with 534 full- or part-time workers) in U.S. workplaces confirmed that 44 percent of the respondents reported that they have worked for an abusive boss. In addition, the study reported that workers ages 18 to 24 are less likely to have encountered an abusive boss (24 percent) than are their older counterparts, who report a higher incident rate (ages 25 to 34: 37 percent; ages 35 to 44: 49 percent; ages 45 to 54: 49 percent; and ages 55 to 64: 56 percent).

College-educated workers report more bullying (47 percent) than those with a high-school education or less (34 percent), while Southern workers (34 percent) are less likely to have experience with an abusive boss than are their Northeastern (56 percent) and Midwestern (48 percent) counterparts. An overwhelming number of the study's participants (64 percent) stated that they believe an abused worker should have the right to sue to recover damages.

U.S. Workplace Bullying Survey (2007)

Similarly, in September 2007, a poll conducted by Zogby International for the Workplace Bullying Institute (consisting of 7,740 online interviews and herein referred to as the "U.S. Workplace Bullying Survey (2007)") found that 37 percent of American workers, an estimated 54 million employees, report being bullied at work. When organizational bystanders are included, bullying affects nearly half (49 percent) of employees in America, or 71.5 million workers.[6]

According to the study, workplace bullying is four times as prevalent as illegal discrimination or harassment. In 62 percent of the cases actually reported, when made aware of the bullying, employers did nothing. Seventy-two percent of the bullies were bosses, and 55 percent of those bullied were rank-and-file employees.

Survey Report by the Society for Human Resource Management and the Ethics Resource Center (2008)

In an interesting study conducted by the Society for Human Resource Management (SHRM) and the Ethics Resource Center,[7] 513 out of 3,000 SHRM members randomly selected to participate in the study responded, yielding a response rate of 19 percent. Overall, in the previous 12 months, approximately three out of 10 HR professionals (32 percent) reported having observed misconduct that they believed violated their organizations' ethics standards, company policy, or the law.

Of the top five types of misconduct witnessed, the most prevalent included abusive or intimidating behavior toward employees (excluding sexual harassment), with 57 percent of the participants reporting that they had witnessed this type of behavior at work. This type of misconduct was closely followed by reports of email and/or Internet abuse (48 percent), misreporting actual time or hours worked (46 percent), behavior that places an employee's interests over the organization's interests (44 percent), and employees calling in sick when they were not (41 percent).

Summary of the Prevalence Studies

These studies confirm what we, as HR professionals, already know: bullying is a common problem that permeates American organizations, resulting in significant costs to its targets, their organizations, and society as a whole.

So Why Do U.S. Employers Allow this Type of Behavior at Work?

Given these statistics, why do employers choose to do so little to protect employees from this devastating mistreatment? Some of the more plausible explanations for the high prevalence rate of bullying in U.S. organizations follow:

- ■ Not Aware of the Problem. Given the fact that 40 percent of targets never report the problem to management, one of the reasons may be that the employer simply is not aware of the problem in many instances.[8]

- No Legislation/No Focus on the Problem. Since bullying is legal in 80 percent of all bullying-related incidents and there is no legislation prohibiting such conduct, employers may fail to take the problem seriously, worrying more about other laws and regulations with which they must currently comply.[9]
- Managers Support Each Other. The fact is that 73 percent of all bullies are managers; as a result, senior management and HR may tend to align themselves with their fellow managers when conflicts arise.[10]
- "Just Following Orders": An unknown percentage of bullies may simply be following orders from higher-ranking officials in the organization, operating as the "corporate henchman" to rid the organization of a perceived "problem employee."
- Fear of Losing Bully: While management may view them as aggressive, arrogant, or difficult, bullies can often also be high performers and therefore perceived to be indispensable to the organization, despite their interpersonal failings and the devastation that they inflict on other employees. As a result, the organization may turn a "blind eye" to the problem in order to protect the bully and keep him or her performing.
- Conflict Avoidance: Senior management and other company leaders are sometimes reluctant to engage in conflict, particularly with individuals whom they perceive to be difficult or powerful (despite their lower rank in the organization). They would rather avoid these types of interpersonal battles, and are often simply afraid to act out of fear that the bully will turn on them.[11]
- Company Minimizes the Problem: Sometimes, employers mistakenly label the mistreatment as "simply an interpersonal conflict that the two individuals must resolve on their own."
- Culture Rewards Aggressive Behaviors: And finally, given the current focus on profits and the "bottom line," many companies are highly aggressive and competitive, and reward those behaviors in employees. As a result, since bullies typically embrace both of these tactics, it often takes awhile for the bully's actions to be viewed as outside of the norm.

Explanations for Bullying Behavior at Work

II Bullies have a personal agenda that is simply 'I'm gonna get you—whatever it takes.' *II*

There have been numerous studies attempting to explain why workplace bullying occurs; however, while the results are inconclusive, they are suggestive. Some of the most widely discussed and probable explanations include the following:

Personalities of the Individuals

In the recent U.S. Workplace Bullying Survey (2007), when asked why bullying happens, respondents reported the following:

- Because of some aspect of the bully's personality: 56 percent;
- Because of the target: 20 percent (13 percent said it was because of some aspect of the target's personality, while 7 percent noted performance deficiencies); and
- Only 14 percent suggested that the bullying may be a systemic issue that is a result of the organizational work environment.

Similarly, other researchers have focused on the personality traits of both the bully and the target, with some studies indicating that certain people are "hard driving" and are easily aroused to hostility. Other studies have suggested that bullies simply appear to believe that it is "better to be feared than loved."

Some have pointed to a "personal deficiency" of the bullies and argued that bullies are disturbed individuals — suggesting that they are power-hungry, enjoy hurting innocent people, and lack normal inhibitions and empathy. According to this line of thinking, the central aim of a bully is simply to intimidate and hurt others.

Other researchers have suggested that bullies are often individuals who are "unwell," are possibly psychotic, and thrive on victimizing others.

These researchers believe that bullies abuse their power at work "knowingly and deliberately." In keeping with the theme of personal shortcomings as a cause of the bullying, still other researchers suggest that bullies are frustrated in their own lives and are deficient in their abilities, therefore using bullying as a "screen" to hide behind.

Economic and Social Trends

Some have suggested that the modern American workplace is "primed for abusive behavior toward workers."[2] Five often-interrelated economic and social trends have been noted by professor and activist David Yamada. These include:

- Growth of the service-sector economy — which requires a great deal of personal interaction; as a result, the more people interact, the more likely it is that personalities will clash and individuals who possess bullying tendencies will act on them;

- Global profit squeeze — which requires U.S. managers and employees to provide more and better goods and services at a lower cost, thereby fueling more stress in the work environment;

- Decline of unionization — resulting in the loss of union representatives as a potential "safety valve" in resolving disputes;

- Diversification of the workforce — with increased differences, one can anticipate more opportunities for conflict and/or aggression to exist; and

- Increased reliance on contingent workers — employees who are only temporary or part-time (generally with no real vested interest in the company) may not care very much about what other people think, resulting in an environment with more conflict and/or abusive behavior.

Diversity/Differences

Others have suggested that the diversity of today's workforce may be a key contributor leading individuals to act aggressively toward others at work. With all of the different cultures, ethnic backgrounds, personalities, beliefs, attitudes, age levels, and gender coming together at work, it is easy to see how these differences (while also often contributing to creative and productive work environments) can contribute to interpersonal conflicts and aggression.

People often attribute hostile motives to those that they perceive as being "different." These differences can stem from race, religion, physical characteristics, weight issues, unusual personality, or sexual orientation, to name just a few. It is important to remember, however, that different treatment of an individual based on "protected characteristics" is discriminatory under federal and state law. As a result, it is necessary to train employees about treating each other with mutual respect and respecting differences in order to keep any inadvertent discriminatory treatment from occurring.

Organizations with Large Numbers of Minority or Low-End Service Workers

From a review of a number of studies, there appears to be a strong correlation between workforces involving a large number of minority or low-end service workers and the presence of bullying. It has been speculated that bullies may find minority workers to be easy targets because they may already face a certain degree of organizational and social isolation from majority groups (perhaps due to their racial or national characteristics). Similarly, employees in low-status service positions may be particularly vulnerable to bullying due to the constant supervision that is a common component of such jobs.

Reward and Recognition Programs

Employers sometimes implicitly offer a positive response to aggression at work by rewarding people who display aggressive behaviors. Frequently, this occurs through promotions, bonuses, or positive recognition, or a combination of these types of rewards. This not only signals to employees that this type of conduct is acceptable, but it also suggests that it is to be commended and imitated (both to the individual bully, as well as to those employees who have witnessed the abusive behavior).

Social learning theory suggests that individuals who operate in a work environment where others are rewarded for aggressive behavior are more likely to engage in similar acts themselves. So when employees see managers acting abusively and disrespectfully toward others, they will conduct themselves similarly.

Aggressive Competition

Consistent with the outcome of reward and recognition programs that implicitly reward inappropriate behaviors (although the organization most certainly does not intend to do so), the workplace environment in the United States may also foster bullying behavior by allowing aggressive competition that "pits individuals against each other." When team-building practices are largely absent, and workers succeed (or fail) through "cut-throat" behavior, the environment is ripe for situations of workplace bullying.

Organizational Culture

Many researchers have suggested that organizational culture plays a large and important role in the manifestation of workplace bullying. In some organizations, bullying and other forms of harassment seem to be more or less accepted as "the way things are done around here." As a result, they can become desensitized to this type of behavior and begin to take it for granted as "normal." This desensitization may lower the cost and perceived danger associated with bullying, allowing the work climate to actually support and encourage these types of behaviors.

If an organization has no policy against bullying or if it does not have training and/or policies that require that all employees be treated with respect and dignity, or regularly fails to deal with interpersonal conflict, employees might legitimately assume that the organization accepts it — what has been referred to as organizational "permission to harass."[3]

It has also been suggested that bullying behaviors may be a result of a belief among managers that workers are most productive when they are pushed by a fear of harassment. This statement implies that bullying and harassment may be viewed as a normal operating method by management in order to achieve organizational productivity. As a result, the bully may come to believe that such behavior is acceptable within the organization's cultural norms. If this occurs, it is highly unlikely that the bully will make any personal effort to temper or restrain his behavior. Similarly, some organizational cultures may even celebrate and/or reward behavior that indicates that a manager is "tough" and "in control."

Stressful Work Conditions

Factors in the physical work environment — such as crowding, uncomfortable temperatures, and noise — may also contribute to employee dissatisfaction, resulting in increased aggression at work. Others have concluded that when employees are working under significant stress and time pressures, the situation just does not allow for the polite "niceties" of business life. As a result, there is more risk for interpersonal conflict that may end up as a bullying situation as the conflict escalates.

Interaction between Individual and Situational Factors

Researchers have confirmed that bullying and other forms of aggression often result from an *interaction between* individual and situational factors. Among the many possible factors that have been suggested, the most prevalent include intense global competition; rapid technological change; major shifts in workforce demographics; downsizing, rightsizing, outsourcing, and restructuring in an effort to reduce costs; employee monitoring, job sharing, and pay cuts that add to employee stress levels; and expanded monitoring and surveillance of employee communications (for example, phone conversations, computer files, email, voice mail messages, and the like).

The rationale is that the individual and the organization may exert mutual influence on each other — that is, an individual may acquire aggressive tendencies in a certain environment, and the work environment and culture may be influenced by the aggressive individual at times as well. That an individual may be influenced to become more aggressive in certain work environments is supported by the hypothesis that some bullying individuals may be "context-specific" bullies, behaving badly at work but more or less normally in other contexts.[4]

Imitation of Other Successful Managers/Leaders

It will come as no surprise that employees tend to model and imitate the behavior and style of managers who are perceived to be "successful." This imitation may also influence the prevalence of bullying. In situations where new managers are socialized into a culture that treats bullying of employees as a "normal" and acceptable way of getting things done, bullying behaviors appear to escalate.

Loyalty to the Organization

Many targets seem to consider complaining about bullying to be an act of "disloyalty" to their supervisor or to the organization. This fact was recently borne out in the U.S. Workplace Bullying Survey (2007) wherein 40 percent of the targets indicated that they never reported the problem to their employer. If loyalty keeps problems from being reported, the organization cannot take action to stop the abuse. As a result, bullying flourishes in environments where employees are extremely loyal and reluctant to speak up about problems.

Significant Times of Organizational Transition

One of the most commonly cited causes for an increase in bullying is the insecure job environment typically brought about by corporate restructuring, outsourcing, downsizing, and possible mergers or acquisitions ahead. Concerns about the future may result in general feelings of uncertainty and powerlessness among employees. As a result, it has been suggested that this insecurity diminishes an employee's sense of power and control, thus creating a stressful environment in which civility and professionalism is replaced by bullying. The reason: managers seek to intimidate and blame employees because of their mutually held fears about the future security of their respective jobs.

It should be noted that employees who feel powerless are more likely to engage in destructive behavior. During such times, employees may try to elevate their own status and perceived value to the organization by attempting to decrease the prestige or standing of other employees by engaging in verbal abuse, spreading rumors, or engaging in other types of negative activities.

Job Insecurity and Chaotic Work Environments

As managerial layers and positions are eliminated (most frequently as a result of restructuring, outsourcing, rightsizing, and downsizing, as well as mergers and acquisitions), promotional opportunities become more limited. At the same time, the workload of individual employees increases. Given more limited resources, competition for promotions and internal opportunities increases, negatively impacting the perception among employees about their future job security.

One of the most common paths to bullying is through job insecurity and organizational chaos. When employees feel threatened with future job loss, they may feel less constrained to act civilly because of reduced expectations of having a continuing relationship with their co-workers in the future. This, in turn, leads to higher pressures and more stress, lowering thresholds for aggression and increasing the potential benefits for a bully to seek to eliminate colleagues and subordinates who now appear to represent a potential "threat" or, in some cases, are perceived to be a "burden" to their department or the organization.

Personality Disorders

There is a growing body of research that has attempted to look at bullying and personality disorders to determine whether or not there is some correlation between the characteristics of those who bully and those who do not.

A pair of researchers in the United Kingdom interviewed and gave personality tests to high-level British executives and compared their profiles with those of criminal psychiatric patients at Broadmoor Prison. Out of 11 personality disorders, they found that three were actually more common in corporate managers than in the disturbed criminal-patients.[5] These included:

- Histrionic personality disorder — including superficial charm, insincerity, and manipulation;
- Narcissistic personality disorder — including grandiosity, self-focused lack of empathy for others, exploitativeness, and independence; and
- Obsessive-compulsive personality disorder — including perfectionism, excessive devotion to work, rigidity, stubbornness, and dictatorial tendencies.

Interestingly, they described the businesspeople as "successful psychopaths" and the criminals as "unsuccessful psychopaths."[6]

In addition to this study in the U.K., several researchers have discussed the relationship between psychopathy and workplace bullying. You may be able to identify specific people in your organization who fit these descriptions:[7]

Bullies react aggressively in response to provocation or perceived insults or slights. It is unclear whether their acts of bullying give them pleasure or are just the most effective way they have learned to get what they want from others. Similar to manipulators, however, psychopathic bullies do not feel remorse, guilt or empathy. They lack insight into their own behavior, and seem unwilling or unable to moderate it, even when it is to their own advantage. Not being able to understand the harm they do to themselves (let alone their victims), psychopathic bullies are particularly dangerous.

Of course, not all bullies are psychopathic, though this may be of little concern to their victims. Bullies come in many psychological and physical sizes and shapes. In many cases, "garden variety" bullies have deep-seated psychological problems, including feelings of inferiority or inadequacy and difficulty in relating to others. Some may simply have learned at an early age that their size, strength, or verbal talent was the only effective tool they had for social behavior. Some of these individuals may be context-specific bullies, behaving badly at work but more or less normally in other contexts. But the psychopathic bully is what he is: a callous, vindictive, controlling individual with little or no empathy or concern for the rights and feelings of the victim, no matter what the context.

Earlier research also confirmed that many bullies have some (or all) of the features of a medically diagnosable personality disorder.

Summary of the Research

There are numerous studies attempting to provide possible explanations about why bullying occurs in our organizations. The empirical investigations have mainly addressed the issue from four aspects: the individual personality of the bully, the individual personality of the target, the role of the organization, plus situational factors.

While researchers and activists may argue or disagree about the reasons for bullying, it is necessary to caution that no single explanation will ever accurately fit each particular bullying situation. While one cause may play a big role in some cases, it may not be present as a factor in others. In the end, we have to look at the broader picture, as each bullying situation is likely to be driven by a *combination* of individual, organizational, and situational factors.

Consequences of Workplace Bullying: The Damages and Costs

II Interestingly, [researchers] have studied this in depth and shown that the financial costs to organizations of assholes far exceeds their benefits. Profits increase when it is rooted out; profits fall when it runs rampant. Bullying is bad for business.[1] *II*

Workplace bullying affects the target, the "organizational bystanders," and the organization, as well as the target's family and friends — each in significant ways. Interestingly, though, the bully is not usually directly affected. The consequences of bullying on each of these parties will be discussed separately below.

To the Target

The research is overwhelmingly consistent in reporting that bullying behavior leads to serious physical and emotional problems for the targets, including damage to their self-esteem and confidence, anxiety, depression, gastrointestinal disorders, headaches, insomnia, exhaustion, poor concentration, and substance abuse. Left untreated and with prolonged exposure, cardiovascular stress-related diseases are also a likely result.

Specifically, persistently abused employees report elevated levels of anxiety and are at higher risk of substance abuse, depression, and heart disease than non-abused workers. Targets often suffer long-term (sometimes permanent) psychological and occupational impairment. Considerable evidence also suggests that bullying is a "crippling and devastating problem."[2] Employees subjected to repeated abuse are also at an increased risk of prolonged duress stress disorder, post-traumatic stress disorder, and suicidal ideation — and even suicide. Some targets are so damaged that they cannot reintegrate back into the workforce, or can do so only after intensive, specialized rehabilitation therapy.

Workplace bullying appears to inflict more severe harm on employees than does sexual harassment.[3] According to a meta-analysis of more than 100 previous studies, the researchers reported that employees who experience bullying, incivility, or interpersonal conflict were more likely to quit their jobs, have lower well-being, be less satisfied with their jobs, and have less satisfying relations with their bosses than employees who were sexually harassed. Targets also reported more job stress, less job commitment, and higher levels of anger and anxiety.

In the previously discussed U.S. Workplace Bullying Survey (2007), 45 percent of targets reported stress-related health problems resulting from the bullying. Based on prior research by the Workplace Bullying Institute (which co-authored the 2007 study), these stress effects included severe anxiety (76 percent), disrupted sleep (71 percent), loss of concentration (71 percent), post-traumatic stress disorder (47 percent), clinical depression (39 percent), and panic attacks (32 percent).

This overwhelming body of evidence convincingly demonstrates a direct association between exposure to an abusive work environment with numerous negative and often severe health consequences, all of which are stress-related. It should be noted, though, that at least some of the reported consequences of bullying — such as ill health, reduced organizational commitment, and decreased productivity — are strongly associated with the target's own subjective evaluation of the situation.

Studies have reported that targets describe the experience of bullying as being a "nightmare," "a battle," or "torture," with the resulting bullying actions making bullied employees "feel like slaves and animals, prisoners, children, and heartbroken lovers."[4] Work-induced trauma has been reported to be "as disruptive of life functioning as trauma induced by war."[5] This research led one of the American originators of the anti-bullying movement, Dr. Gary Namie, to state, "For many bullied targets, the workplace has become a war zone."[6]

Targets are typically directed by their internal Human Resources to seek workers' compensation for their emotional injuries; however, the reality is that cases of stress-related psychological or emotional harm are rarely awarded workers' compensation. Researchers have suggested that employer resistance and insurer obstacles serve to prolong or prevent the target's recovery from the trauma associated with the bullying.

According to the U.S. Workplace Bullying Survey (2007), once bullying begins, it is not likely to stop until the targets are terminated (in 2 percent of cases), voluntarily leave the organization (40 percent), or transfer to another department within the same company (13 percent). When 40 percent of bullied individuals quit their jobs, this represents a preventable loss of 21.6 million employees — at a time when U.S. employers face critical shortages of skilled workers.

To the Organization

In addition to causing stress and social harm to targets, bullying also has significant economic consequences. The U.S. Workplace Bullying Survey (2007) reported that *tangible* costs increase to employers in the following areas:

- Turnover, including costs associated with recruitment, interviewing, and hiring;
- Absenteeism/lost productivity;
- Workers' compensation; and
- Disability insurance, both short- and long-term.

In addition to the tangible costs, the survey reported *intangible* costs affecting employers as a result of workplace bullying that included employee sabotage, difficult recruitment and retention of key employees, and a tarnished reputation as a "Worst Place to Work." The associated costs resulting from potential litigation from a workplace bullying claim must also be considered.

Targets of bullying reportedly take an average of seven days more sick leave per year than those who were neither bullied nor witnessed bullying taking place.[7] In addition to their frequent absences, 46 percent of all targets indicated that they were thinking about leaving their organization.[8]

The costs of bullying to an organization have been estimated at approximately $30,000 to $100,000 per year *for each individual* subjected to bullying.[9] In addition to the out-of-pocket expenses, abusive work environments result in "fear and mistrust, resentment, hostility, feelings of humiliation, withdrawal, 'playing-it-safe' strategies and hiding mistakes,"[10] all of which have their own (though more difficult to quantify) costs.

A study by the National Institute for Occupational Safety and Health (NIOSH) found that stressful working conditions lead to higher levels of absenteeism and turnover and lower motivation and morale.[11] In addition, the mental impact of bullying among the workforce reportedly leads to a loss in employment totaling $19 billion, and a drop in productivity of $3 billion.[12]

According to a cooperative report by the World Health Organization and the International Labour Organization, the drop in productivity caused by stress related to bullying results in $80 billion in lost revenues per year.[13]

Additionally, the American Institute of Stress reported one million workers miss work every day due to stress-related illnesses (a large percentage of which is obviously caused by workplace bullying).[14]

The American Psychological Association estimates that American businesses lose approximately $300 billion per year as a result of the loss of productivity, absenteeism, turnover, and increased medical costs due to increased stress at work created by bullying and other forms of abuse.[15] As a result, individual targets are not the only ones suffering. Organizational profits are also negatively impacted. In combination, these factors hinder America's ability to successfully compete in the global marketplace.

The Corporate Leavers Survey (a study of more than 1,700 participants released in early 2007 by the Level Playing Field Institute)[16] indicated that two million professionals and managers leave their jobs annually, pushed out by "cumulative small comments, whispered jokes, and not-so-funny emails." This unfair treatment, which includes aspects of workplace bullying (most frequently the public humiliation of employees) reportedly costs U.S. employers $64 billion on an annual basis — a price tag nearly equivalent to the 2006 combined revenues of Google, Goldman Sachs, Starbucks, and Amazon.com,[17] or the gross domestic product of the 55th wealthiest country in the world.[18]

Similarly, a Gallup Organization study[19] reported that most workers rate having a caring boss even higher than money or fringe benefits. In interviews with two million employees at 700 different companies, Gallup found that how long employees stay at companies and how productive they are is frequently determined by the quality of their relationship with their immediate supervisor. Given that the primary reason people leave their jobs is dissatisfaction with their supervisor — not their paycheck — this reality has given rise to the oft-repeated remark that "people join companies and leave managers."[20]

To the Bully

Though it may come as a surprise (but maybe not), the bully is negatively affected in just 23 percent of all reported situations — with only 14 percent of bullies actually terminated from their companies as a result of the offensive conduct, and 9 percent remaining employed in the organization but receiving some sort of discipline as a result of the offense.[21]

It may also surprise you to learn that bullies operate with some degree of confidence that they are not likely to be disciplined as a result of their bullying actions. This is in large part because 35 percent of the survey respondents in the U.S. Workplace Bullying Survey indicated that the bully has an "executive sponsor" (which includes senior managers, executives, or company owners who are likely to protect the bully if and when he or she is exposed).[22] Further, 27 percent reported that the bully's colleagues also supported the bully, while 11 percent indicated that their HR department was supportive of the bully as well.

When the problem is reported to the organization, employers either made the problem worse or simply did nothing 62 percent of the time.[23] Specifically, the survey found the following employer responses to a report of bullying:

- 18 percent actually made the problem worse,
- 44 percent took no action at all, and
- Only 32 percent actually helped (or at least tried to assist) in resolving the conflict.

With this abysmal type of response, it is no wonder that targets report these types of problems to managers only 40 percent of time.[24]

To the "Organizational Bystanders"

Observers of bullying report higher levels of generalized stress than those who have not experienced or observed bullying taking place. Similarly, approximately one in five witnesses have stated that they considered leaving their organization as a result of having witnessed bullying.[25] It has been said that a "climate of fear" exists within an organization characterized by frequent bullying.[26] This claim was supported by the target's affirmative confirmation of statements such as "workers too scared to report" (95 percent), "the bully has done this before" (84 percent), and "management knew about it" (73 percent).

Researchers have also found increased symptoms of depression, anxiety, and psychosomatic complaints in those who were not the actual victims of the abuse, but who were simply witnesses present in the work environment.

To the Target's Friends and Family

In addition to the damage to individuals in the workplace, it should not be forgotten that the friends and family of a target are often affected as well. Relationships suffer, and normal family functioning is frequently disrupted, often resulting in either divorce or estrangement.

Existing Legal and Policy Protections

// Bullying is the sexual harassment of 20 years ago; everybody knows about it, but nobody wants to admit it.[1] *//*

Important Disclaimer: This material is provided for informational purposes only and is not intended as a substitute for the advice of an attorney.

As HR practitioners (usually working closely with legal counsel), you are generally the internal professionals called upon to manage and make sense of existing laws, as well as to monitor and prepare for new legislation. Among the many duties that are associated with the management of these sorts of people-related legal issues, you are the organizational "insiders" that are called upon to develop manager and employee training, corporate policies, employee communications, and other organizational strategies.

This chapter will begin with a comparison of sexual harassment and workplace bullying, noting the similarities that the two forms of misconduct share, as well as the manner in which both the law and the public have responded to discussions about prohibiting such conduct. The chapter will also cover the key laws, both in the United States and internationally, that currently may be relevant to situations of workplace bullying. It will also discuss the limited case law that exists, promising legal theories, and the policies of several early-adopting employers.

Bullying as Compared to the Evolution of Sexual Harassment Protections

Researchers in this area have compared workplace bullying to the concerns expressed about sexual harassment 20 years ago.[2] The similarities are startling:

- Both problems were shrouded in silence before being brought to public attention;
- Both actions create a "hostile work environment";
- Both involve the abuse of organizational power by a specific individual;
- Both are different forms of work-related harassment;[3]
- Neither are "accidental" — they are intentional, aggressive behaviors;
- In both, the perpetrator and the target are on the employer's payroll;
- In both, the trauma experienced by the targets is caused by going to work;
- In both, targets are often initially blamed as being "thin-skinned" such that they must deserve their fate;
- Both have severe consequences for the personal well-being and job satisfaction of the target;
- Both require significant investments of organizational time and resources to identify, correct, and prevent; and
- Both result in increased turnover and health care costs, as well as damage to the employer's reputation if the issue is reported publicly, making employee recruitment and retention more difficult.

Statistically, bullying is far more prevalent than sexual harassment, workplace violence, or racial discrimination.[4] In fact, the recent U.S. Workplace Bullying Survey suggests that it is *four time*s as prevalent as either illegal discrimination or harassment![5]

Existing Legal Protections in the United States

Lawsuits about workplace bullying have been somewhat rare (so far), but they do happen. In those cases when a target has finally "had it" and is ready to take legal action, they typically seek out an employment lawyer. Oftentimes, what they find is that many of the few attorneys who specialize in harassment and/or workplace abuse issues are not interested in their case.

Attorneys who do counsel targets of workplace bullying need some legal justification for filing a lawsuit. Consistent with the law's historic reluctance to regulate the everyday employment arena, workplace bullying has not yet been fully recognized and addressed by the American legal system.

In most cases, though, the laws that are most widely thought to be most relevant to bullying include Title VII of the Civil Rights Act, the Americans with Disabilities Act, the Age Discrimination in Employment Act, or the False Claims Act. In addition, there may be protections afforded by federal and state labor statutes, collective bargaining agreements, and retaliation and whistleblowing statutes. This section will provide you with an overview of these key federal laws; however, given that there is very little case law in this area, the success of their application to this phenomenon has not really been tested much, so it remains uncertain.

Title VII of the Civil Rights Act of 1964

Currently, Title VII of the Civil Rights Act of 1964 permits relief for members of protected classes based upon a theory of a "hostile work environment." "Protected classes" include individuals who possess legally protected characteristics such as race, color, sex (including pregnancy), religion, and national origin,[6] and who work for companies with at least 15 employees. Age and disability are also considered to be protected classes; however, they are covered by different laws that will be discussed separately.

The criterion for determining "hostile work environment" covers a workplace where "intimidation and ridicule are so severe that they alter the conditions of the victim's employment and create an abusive working environment that interferes with performance" and "a reasonable person finds this behavior hostile and the victim perceives the environment to be abusive."[7] It may come as a huge surprise to you (as it does to most people) that the law does not, however, protect victims of bullying behavior unless they are a member of one of the designated "protected classes" who might be able to establish a claim against their employer under existing discrimination laws (except in same-sex and same-race harassment, where the protections do not apply).

Seldom is this the case. In only 20 percent of bullying cases does the target have "protected class status" that would qualify them to file a discrimination or harassment complaint under existing law.[8] As a result, it is not enough for an individual to file a lawsuit claiming that "My boss bullied me" or "My boss harassed me." In order to state a valid cause of action under current discrimination laws, the target would have to claim "My boss harassed me because of my sex ... or because of my age ... or my race" and so on. This is what is referred to as the current "gap" in existing U.S. law.

Americans with Disabilities Act of 1993

Another federal statute, the Americans with Disabilities Act of 1993 (ADA),[9] may offer some relief when abusive behavior has caused or exacerbated a recognized mental disability. Research by civil rights attorney and former law professor Susan Stefan has demonstrated that claims under the ADA by employees involving psychiatric disabilities tend to fit into one of four common profiles:

1. Employees who had worked satisfactorily for an extended period of time until the appointment of a new supervisor and whose claims clearly arose from escalating interpersonal difficulties with their supervisors.

2. Employees whose psychiatric disabilities arose from other work environment issues, including women who were sexually harassed; individuals subjected to hostile work environments as a result of disability, gender, race, or sexual preferences; whistleblowers; and people whose disabilities were related to other claims of employer abuse or unfair treatment.

3. Employees whose disabilities were related to increasing stress, increased hours on the job, or the demands of new positions or new responsibilities.

4. Employees disciplined for misconduct, usually sexual harassment, who claimed that their behavior resulted from a mental disability or that being disciplined showed that their employer perceived them as being mentally disabled.

The ADA protects workers from discrimination due to a target's physical or mental impairment or learning disability that substantially limits one or more of the major life activities (e.g., walking, working, etc.). It must be noted, however, that a bully may also have a claim under the ADA if he or she suffers adverse employment action.

The ADA requires employers to make a "reasonable accommodation" for employees with disabilities, provided that the accommodation does not impose an "undue hardship" for the employer. However, many bullied employees lose their ADA cases "because abuse and stress are seen as simply intrinsic to employment, as invisible and inseparable from conditions of employment as sexual harassment was twenty years ago."[10]

Recent amendments to the ADA were signed into law by President George W. Bush and became effective on January 1, 2009. A significant ramification of these changes is that even if an employee is simply "perceived" to have mental or emotional impairments (but does not, in fact, actually have a covered disability), then it is possible that an ADA claim may still be initiated if he or she is bullied at work.

Age Discrimination in Employment Act of 1967

Another potential avenue of relief for a bullied employee is under the federal Age Discrimination in Employment Act of 1967 (commonly referred to as the ADEA). However, in order for this law to apply, the target must be a member of the "protected class" of individuals who are 40 years of age or older. If he or she falls into this category, he or she is protected from employment discrimination based on age. The ADEA's protections apply to both employees and job applicants, and make it unlawful to discriminate against a person because of his or her age with respect to any term, condition, or privilege of employment, including hiring, firing, promotion, layoff, compensation, benefits, job assignments, and training.[11]

It is also unlawful to retaliate against an individual for opposing employment practices that discriminate based on age or for filing an age discrimination charge, testifying, or participating in any way in an investigation, proceeding, or litigation under the ADEA. However, under the ADEA, it is permissible for employers to favor older workers based on their age even when doing so adversely affects workers younger than 40. The ADEA applies to employers with at least 20 employees, including state and local governments. It also applies to employment agencies and labor organizations, as well as to the federal government.

Occupational Safety and Health Act

The Occupational Safety and Health Act (OSH Act) may also offer some additional protection to victims of workplace bullying. In its *Fact Sheet on Workplace Violence*, OSHA indicates that protected workplace violence "can range from threats and verbal abuse to physical assaults and homicide...."[12] In the OSH Act's general duty clause, employers are required to provide "a safe and healthful workplace" for all workers covered by the OSH Act. If an employer fails to meet its requirements in this regard, it can be cited for an OSHA violation.

A failure to implement the anti-violence suggestions that are outlined in the *Fact Sheet* is not, in itself, a violation of the general duty clause. As a result, it appears that the protections available under this regulation may be somewhat limited. However, the OSH Act's mandate "to provide safe and healthful working conditions" for employees could be used as a strong rationale to a company's management team as a basis for the need to develop effective HR programs to safeguard employees from bullying.

False Claims Act

The False Claims Act is commonly called the "whistleblower" act because it protects employees who speak out about a company when it is making false monetary claims against the federal and state government, charging them for goods or services not rightfully rendered, or involved in criminal activities (for example, money laundering, embezzlement, bribery, kickbacks, drug trafficking, and income tax evasion).[13]

Federal and State Labor Statutes and Collective Bargaining Agreements

Federal and state labor statutes (specifically the National Labor Relations Act) and collective bargaining agreements may also be sources of protection for bullied employees. The key distinction is whether or not the individual is covered by a collective bargaining agreement (the provisions of which will largely define the individual's substantive and procedural rights). However, it is possible that even non-union employees may have limited recourse under federal or state laws.

Free-Speech Protections

Although public employee speech is protected by the First Amendment, those protections apply only to the degree that the speech addresses matters of public concern. It would appear that employee speech related to one's official work duties (which would encompass an employee's internal complaints about bullying) would not be covered by the First Amendment. This is a difficult hurdle to surpass for most typical bullying situations; however, it could have some relevance to whistleblower or retaliation situations.

For private employees, there is little hope of invoking a constitutional right to free speech, given a body of case law that holds that employees enjoy no federal or state constitutional protection against incursions on free speech by private parties.

Retaliation and Whistleblowing

Survey data collected by the Workplace Bullying Institute suggests that a leading motivation behind workplace bullying is due to retaliation for engaging in some type of whistleblowing or for rebuffing sexual advances. Engaging in union organizing activity may also encourage retaliatory behavior. As a result, the anti-retaliation provisions of various protective employment statutes may be applicable to these types of situations. In addition, retaliatory actions that result in an individual's termination of employment, either actual or constructive, may raise other statutory violations, including the possibility of a violation of the public policy exception to "at will" employment or other wrongful discharge claims (see the *Constructive Discharge* section in this chapter for more information about this issue).

Employee Benefits

The current complexity of available employee benefits does not provide bullied employees with any real safety net. If anything, it probably serves to exacerbate the stress and health-related problems typically faced by many bullying targets. The most commonly available employee benefits will be discussed below.

Workers' Compensation Statutes

Workers' compensation statutes generally provide replacement income and medical expenses to employees who are injured or become ill due to their jobs. However, such claims are more likely to be contested where the injury is a psychological one, and often this will trigger an inquiry into the employee's past emotional state. In addition, workers' compensation statutes in many states do not provide coverage for stress-related illnesses.

Generally, in most circumstances, workers' compensation pays relatively modest amounts and prevents the employee or his or her dependents from suing the employer or co-workers. However, there are some exceptions to these exclusivity provisions. For example, in California, an injured employee may bring a civil action against another employee when an injury is proximately caused by the "willful and unprovoked physical act of aggression of the other employee."[14] Use of this theory, however, would require an overt physical act, which is uncommon in bullying situations.

Health Insurance

Many employer health care plans provide limited or no coverage for mental health counseling and treatment. Targets of bullying who leave their jobs stand to lose employer-supported health insurance, and the costs of paying for continued health coverage under COBRA may be prohibitive.

Unemployment Insurance

A target that has been terminated from employment may have a claim for unemployment compensation. To be eligible, the target must prove that he or she is out of work through no fault of his or her own. However, bullied employees who leave their jobs instead of continuing to face abuse may encounter great difficulty obtaining unemployment benefits.

In most states, individuals who resign from employment voluntarily are typically ineligible for these benefits. To be successful in establishing their right to receive unemployment benefits, the target must establish that he or she left employment due to "intolerable conditions" that the employer refused to correct after being notified of the problem.

Social Security or Employer-Sponsored Disability Benefits

If a target has worked long enough to meet the eligibility requirements, disability benefits may be available to those who are medically certified as "disabled" (either permanently or partially) through their company's pension or disability plan, or through the federal Social Security system. However, for an individual who is suffering from psychiatric illness, it is often difficult to establish eligibility.

Government Agency Protections

National Institute for Occupational Safety and Health

Although the National Institute for Occupational Safety and Health (NIOSH) is not a policy-making body, it does serve as the federal government's primary research arm about workplace safety. NIOSH has held conferences and participated in research about workplace bullying, both of which validate the government's view that bullying is a social and economic problem in the United States. In addition, NIOSH's research may help to inform the discussions about future regulatory initiatives.

Sparse Case Law

While there are at least some statutory protections in place, the case law is still rather sparse. One landmark bullying case is a 2005 Indiana case in which a heart surgeon was sued by a perfusionist for assault, intentional infliction of emotional distress, and tortious interference with business relations over an incident in the operating room. The surgeon, purportedly angry about the plaintiff's complaints about him to the hospital administration, "aggressively and rapidly advanced on the plaintiff with clenched fists, piercing eyes, beet-red face, popping veins, and screaming and swearing at him."

The plaintiff backed up against a wall and put his hands up, believing that the defendant was going to hit him, "that he was going to smack the s**t out of me or do something." Then the defendant suddenly stopped, turned, and stormed past the plaintiff and left the room, momentarily stopping to declare to the plaintiff "you're finished, you're history."

The jury awarded the plaintiff $325,000 on the assault count, but the Court of Appeals reversed that result and ordered a new trial. Then, in a 4-1 decision on April 8, 2008, the Indiana Supreme Court overruled the Court of Appeals and reinstated the trial court award.[15]

In language that will likely be used in future workplace bullying cases, the Indiana Supreme Court said:

> ... The phrase "workplace bullying," like other general terms used to characterize a person's behavior, is an entirely appropriate consideration in determining the issues before the jury. As evidenced by the trial court's questions to counsel during pre-trial proceedings, *workplace bullying could "be considered a form of intentional infliction of emotional distress."* (emphasis added)

This is widely regarded as the first time a workplace bullying case has been heard and decided in the United States.

Promising Legal Theories

Intentional Infliction of Emotional Distress

Even prior to the 2008 Indiana decision, the preferred avenue for employees seeking relief for abusive treatment in the workplace has been the state common law tort claim of intentional infliction of emotional distress, typically referenced as "IIED."[16] This decision has undoubtedly confirmed IIED as the preferred litigation strategy for future cases.

The tort of IIED is typically defined as follows:

1. The wrongdoer's conduct must be intentional or reckless,
2. The conduct must be outrageous and intolerable in that it offends against the generally accepted standards of decency and morality,
3. There must be a causal connection between the wrongdoer's conduct and the emotional distress, and
4. The emotional distress must be severe.

Typically, plaintiffs have sought to impose liability for IIED on both their employers and the specific individuals (often supervisors) who engaged in the alleged conduct; however, historically, these types of cases have been difficult to win. The biggest hurdle to proving the tort is demonstrating that the conduct complained of is "so atrocious that it passes the bounds of decency and is utterly intolerable to the civilized community."[17] However, this potential cause of action does, at least, provide a possible avenue of relief for victims of workplace bullying.

Intentional Interference with the Employment Relationship

Another tort theory that potentially may be invoked as a response to workplace bullying is intentional interference with the employment relationship. This tort is defined as follows:

1. The plaintiff had an employment contract with an employer,
2. A third party knowingly induced the employer to break that contract,
3. The third party's interference was both intentional and improper in motive or means, and
4. The plaintiff was harmed by the third party's actions.[18]

In *Eserhut v. Heister*,[19] a Washington court found that an employee can be liable for intentionally interfering with a co-worker's contractual relationship with the employer, resulting in the co-worker's resignation. Under the facts in *Eserhut*, three of the plaintiff's co-workers isolated him "by not communicating with and socially ostracizing him." The plaintiff claimed his co-workers' treatment of him caused sleeplessness, depression, and indigestion. The court concluded that if the plaintiff could prove the elements of the tort, "the co-employees can be held liable for intentionally interfering with [the plaintiff's] employment."

Other Intentional Torts

In addition, common law torts such as assault, battery, and false imprisonment may be applicable to certain bullying cases; however, unless the case is accompanied by severe physical and/or mental harm, it is likely to be impractical for a victim to successfully bring such an action. In rare cases, defamation claims may be viable as well, but the pre-emptive effect of workers' compensation statutes must be considered.

Constructive Discharge

For severely bullied employees, the most frequent response is to leave their jobs. From a legal standpoint, this raises the question of whether these so-called "voluntary" departures can be construed as constructive discharges for purposes of alleging a wrongful discharge claim.

Constructive discharge is typically defined as a voluntary termination of employment by an employee where working conditions were such that "an objective, reasonable person would find them so intolerable that voluntary termination is the only reasonable alternative."[20] Although workplace bullying and the legal definition of constructive discharge seemingly go hand in hand, courts and agencies vary widely on how narrowly or broadly constructive discharge should actually be construed.

Breach of Contract Claims

As you may have seen occur in your own organization, employer policies against workplace harassment have become more expansive during the past decade. As a result, there is also the potential for a breach of contract claim. Policies that do not just prohibit unlawful harassment but prohibit "all forms of harassment" in the workplace could become the basis for a breach of contract lawsuit by an employee victimized by a bully at work, so be sure to seek legal counsel *before* making any changes to your corporate policies in this regard.

Employer Policies

While the vast majority of employers in the United States have implemented policies prohibiting harassment based on "protected class" status (for example, race, sex, age, national origin, religion, disability, etc.), not as many explicitly include bullying or other forms of abusive workplace behaviors.[21] Although many companies may be considering the possibility, only a small handful of employers, including Goodwill-Southern California (in Los

Angeles),[22] Graniterock (in Watsonville, California),[23] the Oregon Department of Transportation,[24] and the Oregon Department of Environmental Quality,[25] have publicly confirmed their stance on the issue so far.

The Goodwill policy was implemented in 2004 as an "interpersonal misconduct" policy, defining the prohibited conduct as follows: "interpersonal misconduct is an individual's behavior that bullies, demeans, intimidates, ridicules, insults, frightens, persecutes, exploits, and/or threatens a targeted individual and would be perceived as such by a reasonable person."[26]

Under the policy, a person can be terminated or moved to another location; however, typically employees are given a chance to receive coaching or training in management techniques first. A one-time act would not generally rise to the level of prohibited conduct, as Goodwill's policy seeks to put an end to an "ongoing pattern" of abuse. However, when the misconduct is clearly intentional, counseling is generally bypassed in favor of immediate termination.

Four times a year, Goodwill leaders reportedly include information with employee pay stubs about available hotlines for them to report issues related to:

■ Being bullied or harassed at work,
■ Financial misbehavior, or
■ Stealing.

The hotlines are answered by counselors who are not Goodwill staff members.

In addition, when new employees are hired, they undergo a two-day orientation on personnel procedures, including a discussion about the company's workplace bullying policy. Also, employees who exemplify positive aspects of the company's Respect, Integrity, Service, Excellence (RISE) values are recognized at quarterly staff meetings.

During the first year of the policy's implementation, the organization reportedly did fire several employees who violated the policy, both at the senior level in retail and also at the store manager level. Goodwill's president and chief executive officer was quoted as stating: "We believe people should perform the duties of their job, but that can be done in a respectful manner, without bullying."[27]

Graniterock, a construction-materials distributor, recently added non-discriminatory bullying to its list of prohibited conduct in the workplace (which already included harassment based on gender, ethnicity, and other required protections). Its policy specifically prohibits "unnecessary and rude behavior intended to be offensive and cause emotional distress, including 'workplace bullying.'"[28]

The Oregon Department of Transportation policy, written by its Office of Civil Rights, strives to stop harassment of all kinds. It specifically prohibits:

> ... an intimidating, hostile or abusive work environment. It may be sexual, racial, based on national origin, age, disability, religions or a person's sexual orientation. It may also encompass other forms of hostile, intimidating, threatening, humiliating, or violent behaviors which are not necessarily illegal discrimination, but are nonetheless prohibited by this Policy ... workplace harassment can also be verbal or physical behavior which is derogatory, abusive, disparaging, "bullying," threatening, or disrespectful, even if unrelated to a legally protected status.[29]

At the Oregon Department of Environmental Quality, labor (AFSCME) and management recently adopted an extensive "anti-mobbing policy" to ensure that employees are provided "an emotionally safe, respectful work environment, free of intimidation, hostility, harassment, and other mobbing behaviors."[30]

Instead of implementing a specific anti-bullying policy, though, some management attorneys simply recommend updating the company's harassment policy to address "workplace bullying" without actually using those two words.[31] Essentially, what an organization would say is, *"Our policy is that all employees are entitled to a workplace where you are not harassed for any reason."*

The reason for this is concern that a specific anti-bullying policy could potentially set employers up for a new employee cause of action. Why? The courts are increasingly holding that written employment policies are enforceable as contractual agreements. As a result, you are strongly encouraged to include legal counsel from the beginning in any discussions about the possible development of an anti-bullying strategy or policy for your organization.

Existing International Protections

Anti-Bullying Statutes

In 1993, Sweden became the first country to establish an anti-bullying ordinance. Within the past five years, Australia, France, the United Kingdom, Finland, Italy, Ireland, and Germany have followed suit. In some of these countries, references to workplace bullying can be found in judicial and administrative decisions as well.

Effective as of June 2004, Quebec, Canada, incorporated changes to its Labour Standards Act, which now renders "psychological harassment" illegal. That term is defined as:

> ... any vexatious behaviour in the form of repeated and hostile or unwanted conduct, verbal comments, actions or gestures that affect an employee's dignity or psychological or physical integrity and that result in a harmful work environment for the employee.[32]

The Quebec legislation further provides that "a single serious incidence of such behaviour" can also constitute psychological harassment "where it has a lasting harmful effect on an employee." In addition, the Canadian Safety Council suggests that employers establish anti-bullying policies in their employee handbooks that identify bullying as "unacceptable behavior."[33]

European Union Protections

In Europe, the International Labour Organization (ILO) and the European Union (EU) have both publicly acknowledged that bullying is "a serious workplace problem." In fact, in April 2007, the EU's "social partnership organizations"[34] signed a "framework agreement" regarding workplace violence and harassment at work. Those terms are used by the EU as being synonymous with workplace bullying. Harassment is defined as occurring when "one or more worker or manager are repeatedly and deliberately abused, threatened, and/or humiliated in circumstances relating to work."

This agreement calls for businesses to train managers and workers to reduce incidences of harassment and violence in the workplace, to draft policies explaining that harassment and violence will not be tolerated, and to set out procedures by which investigation into complaints or incidences of violence and harassment will be conducted.

The agreement also contains suggested procedures for investigation and management of complaints. The target date for the EU's member organizations to comply with the framework agreement's objective is April 2010.

Summary of Existing Legal Protections

Despite this recitation of various laws that may prove to be relevant to a bullying complaint, the bottom line, is this: as long as the target of the bullying abuse is not a member of a "protected class," is not physically or mentally disabled, and is not whistleblowing, *there really are no current legal protections for employees in the United States against workplace bullying.*

Legislation on the Horizon

*❚❚*It's laughable that businesses hold bullies accountable. Um, no, they don't. If they did, there wouldn't have been an explosion of targets working to get legislation and others who are speaking about the abuse in the last 2-3 years. I can only hope businesses/public entities hold bullies accountable. Alas, that is not reality and thus, legislation needs to happen to compel behavior as we have unfortunately seen over and over again.[1]*❚❚*

Several recent incidence studies (discussed at length in Chapter 4) have confirmed the pervasiveness of the problem, suggesting that bullying is systemic in American business environments. As a result, it can be anticipated that this type of behavior will likely be hard to change. Though workplace bullying is not yet illegal in all situations, a growing number of U.S. researchers and activists have voiced their view that *"it is time to address this concern."*[2]

The degree, gravity, and regularity of workplace bullying may require law or policy changes, or both. Just as sexually harassing behavior at work was first deemed unacceptable by society and then codified into law, workplace bullying appears to be on a similar trajectory in the United States.

The "Healthy Workplace Bill" — A Proposed Model Act

Employees are not currently protected against workplace bullying unless they are a member of a "protected class" with a right to sue under existing discrimination laws (referred to as "the gap" in legal protection). To bridge this "gap," a model piece of legislation has been proposed that would make workplace bullying illegal for *all* employees, regardless of whether or not the targeted individual is a member of a "protected class." This has also been referred to as "status-blind" protection.

Known as the "Healthy Workplace Bill,"[3] the proposed legislation is intended to provide a legal incentive for U.S. employers to prevent and respond to the mistreatment of employees at work. It is also intended to provide legal redress for employees who have been harmed — psychologically, physically, or economically — by being deliberately subjected to an abusive work environment.[4]

The research and background for this proposed legislation was authored by David Yamada, a professor of law at the Suffolk University Law School in Boston, and strongly supported by the Workplace Bullying Institute.

The proposed legislation would specifically make it an unlawful employment practice to subject an employee to an "abusive work environment," which is defined as "a workplace where an employee is subjected to abusive conduct that is so severe that it causes physical or psychological harm to the employee."

The bill defines abusive conduct precisely — it is clearly not about "incivility" or other minor workplace incidents. As defined in the bill:

> Abusive conduct is conduct of an employer or employee in the workplace, *with malice*, that a reasonable person would find hostile, offensive, and unrelated to an employer's legitimate business interests. In considering whether abusive conduct is present, a trier of fact should weight the severity, nature, and frequency of the conduct ... which may include ... verbal or physical conduct that a reasonable person would find threatening, intimidating or humiliating; or the gratuitous sabotage or undermining of a person's work performance. A single act normally will not constitute abusive conduct, unless especially severe and egregious.

The model act prohibits only severe, health-harming mistreatment for which there is sufficient evidence provided by a competent physician or supported by competent expert evidence at trial.

It also specifies that an employer is vicariously liable for a violation committed by its employee, and would also make the bullying manager directly liable to the complaining target for the unlawful employment practice.

Employers could avoid liability for the actions of the bully based on two affirmative defenses:

- When the employer has exercised reasonable care to prevent and promptly correct the abusive conduct and the employee unreasonably failed to take advantage of the corrective opportunities provided by the employer; or
- When negative employment decisions (for example, terminations, demotions, or punitive transfers) are consistent with legitimate business interests, or with the employee's poor performance, or illegal or unethical activity.[5]

The bill would also make it an unlawful employment practice to retaliate against an employee because the employee has opposed an unlawful employment practice under the bill, or has made a charge, testified, assisted, or participated in an investigation or proceeding under the bill. It would be enforceable solely by a private right of action (which would authorize injunctive relief and would limit an employer's liability for emotional distress to $25,000 where an unlawful employment practice does not result in a negative employment decision). In addition, the employer could not be held liable for punitive damages in such situations either.

The bill would also provide that an aggrieved employee can elect to seek compensation under the bill *or* the workers' compensation remedy — but not both. Actions could be brought only privately, as there is no state regulation that would apply. In other words, the bill explicitly requires that targets make a substantial financial investment in their case to move it forward, and the state is given no enforcement role. This is an important point, as there is no new government bureaucracy that will be created or funded as a result of enactment (which rebuts many of the concerns expressed about the legislation so far).

Ultimately, then, the goal of the proposed legislation is to protect employees by providing them with legal redress when they have been harmed by being deliberately subjected to an abusive work environment. It is also intended to provide incentives for employers to develop internal policies and enforcement in response to workplace bullying, but it is not intended to punish them.

Proposed State and Local Legislation

In 2003, a California state legislator filed a bill titled "A Model Act to Provide Legal Redress for Targets of Workplace Bullying, Abuse and Harassment, Without Regard to Protected Class Status."[6] It marked the first time in the history of American employment law that a bill designed primarily to combat the phenomenon of workplace bullying had been introduced in a major legislative body. Shortly afterward, similar legislation was introduced in the state legislatures of Oklahoma and Oregon. These bills were nearly verbatim adoptions of the model Healthy Workplace Bill.

In 2004, voters in the Amherst, Massachusetts, legislative district overwhelmingly approved a ballot measure instructing their state representative to introduce legislation that funds a state-wide study of workplace bullying and requires employers to develop policies concerning workplace bullying.[7]

Citizens of Hampshire, Massachusetts, voted to approve a public policy question that declared "workplace psychological harassment to be an occupational health issue" and required employers of 50 or more employees to have an anti-bullying policy in place before December 31, 2005.[8] At this juncture, however, no state has actually adopted this anti-bullying protection, although bills have been introduced in 16 states since 2003. In addition, as of July 2008, 16 states have formed grassroots groups to actively promote the proposed Healthy Workplace legislation.[9]

Concerns about Mandatory Legislation

Concerns expressed about the bills proposed to-date include criticisms that they are "short on specifics," such as exactly what would constitute an abusive work environment.[10] Groups like the U.S. Chamber of Commerce have suggested that employers already have an economic incentive to take steps to prevent bullying at work, given the cost and time associated with litigation. The Chamber has argued that employers do not need more regulation; that the bill is too subjective, will be too costly, and will kill new job activity; and that there are already laws at the federal level, and in many states, that protect people against sexual harassment and discrimination based on gender, race, pregnancy, physical and mental disability, as well as religion.

While a number of employment lawyers have confirmed the view that management does need to take proactive steps to address bullying, they have also openly expressed concerns that anti-bullying legislation is "ripe for abuse" and will expose employers to unnecessary litigation. They fear that employees who cannot handle valid, work-related criticism from their supervisors will interpret such negative feedback as harassment or bullying, turning the whole incident into a "slippery slope" very quickly. For example, when a frustrated boss raises his voice at an employee who continues to report to work late, will that be interpreted as meeting the definition of workplace bullying, or is it simply "good management?"

Similarly, other management lawyers have expressed concerns about creating a new cause of action for behaviors that are difficult to define, suggesting that "... the law is a very blunt instrument. It doesn't do well at making nuanced distinctions."[11] What one employee might consider bullying, another employee might not, while a third individual might view it altogether differently as well. The fear is that these differences of opinion about what bullying even is will put a tremendous burden on employers to guess what a jury down the road might consider to be prohibited conduct.

Given that the current legal protections only prohibit abusive behavior based on "protected characteristics," other lawyers have expressed a concern that passing legislation like this "would mean now there's going to be legislation affecting the way people can behave in the workplace."[12] As suggested by one lawyer apparently exasperated by the idea of anti-bullying legislation on the horizon:

> Why do companies need a policy that regulates conduct that is not illegal? Do we really need a policy that tells employees we want them to be nice? If such a policy existed, would it really have any effect whatsoever on the goons in the workplace? My whole problem with the anti-bullying movement is that I don't know how to train people to be *nice*.[13] (emphasis added)

Another lawyer voiced his view that until such time as bullying is illegal, it should be treated as a performance-related issue, not as a policy matter. He laid out his case for this position as follows:

> I am against anything that gives this movement any credibility whatsoever. Implementing anti-bullying policies does just that. Bullying should be addressed just like any other performance problem, in a performance review. Otherwise ... the market corrects itself. Companies that foster bullies will have a revolving-door workforce, which will ultimately hurt productivity and the bottom line. So there is no confusion, I am not in favor of bullying. However, I'm also not in favor of legislation or policies that attempt to address it as a workplace evil.[14]

Confirming this anti-bullying policy stance, other lawyers have suggested:

> ... corporate anti-bullying policies would make every disciplinary situation open for debate. Employers would be required to investigate, and when there are emotions, things are remembered differently. People can view actions as harassment when, in fact, it is nothing more than getting the job done.[15]

Many employment lawyers tend to ignore or minimize the need to deal with behaviors like bullying because such behaviors are not yet explicitly illegal. They look at a conflict situation strictly from the perspective "Is it legal or not?" That view, however, misses the entire point. The behavior may be legal, but it is not a good business practice and must be stopped and, if anyone has the skills and role to deal with the problem, Human Resources is the group to actively take steps to end such abusive behavior at work.

David Yamada, the attorney who authored the "Healthy Workplace Bill" (and is a strong proponent of the need for legislation), has indicated that it is likely that the issue of workplace bullying will continue to be discussed by the public and organizations. He suggests that the issue will continue to "[work] its way into the language of employee relations."[16] Though some anti-bullying activists have publicly expressed doubts about the adoption of the legislation in the near-term, there have been a number of significant changes during the past year (e.g. a new political administration, the economic crisis, numerous public accounts of corporate ethical breaches, etc.) that may conspire to create a more favorable climate for workplace bullying legislation.

"Tough Boss" or Workplace Bully?

// What you call sabotage, I call competition.
What you call conniving deception, I call savvy ambition.
What you call abuse and harassment, I call shrewd gamesmanship.
What you call record-keeping, I call "Hoover files."
And, that's the workplace. It's brutal. It ain't for sissies.
Just play the game.[1] //

In the spring of 2008, the author commenced a research study with the aim of generating a current understanding of the issue of workplace bullying in American organizations (both what it is and what it is not), and how it can be distinguished from situations where a manager is simply operating as a "tough boss."[2] Believed to be the first of its kind, this study provided some unique insights about the issue of workplace bullying from the unique perspective of HR professionals.

Interviews were conducted with 20 experienced HR practitioners located primarily in the Southeastern region of the United States.[3] As such, these interviews provided many examples of how HR professionals identify, experience, and describe the phenomenon of workplace bullying — both as a target of such abuse on a personal level, and also as observers of the experience in their professional HR role.

Key Characteristics of a Workplace Bully

HR practitioners noted the following key characteristics of a workplace bully:

- Misuse of power and authority — to describe the bully's apparent flagrant disregard for following the policies and procedures of the organization;
- Personally-focused and self-interested — to describe the fact that the bully's actions are personally-directed, typically motivated by the bully's own self-interest, and not the furtherance of the goals of the organization;

- Subject to emotional outbursts — to describe the bully's irrational and unpredictable responses that are frequently out of proportion to the situation at hand; and
- Actions perceived as inconsistent and unfair — to describe the bully's tendency to make inconsistent judgments based on his or her own assessment of the situation, without regard to the organization's practices or policies.

"Negative" Acts of a Workplace Bully

In addition, HR professionals noted that workplace bullies commonly engage in work-related acts that are perceived as overwhelmingly *negative*. These included:

- Intimidation — to describe acts that involved behavior which created fear and anxiety among employees;
- Threats — to describe verbal, physical, and economic statements suggesting some type of loss (for example, pay cuts, possible job termination, loss of bonus monies, etc.);
- Exploitation — to describe actions that took advantage of employee weakness and/or vulnerabilities;
- Controlling — to describe actions the bully took to control the activities or behavior of others;
- Humiliation/Embarrassment — to describe actions that involved the public berating or belittling of someone that is intended to cause the target to feel shame or embarrassment;
- Failure to Communicate — to describe acts of one-sided conversations, not listening, or withholding work-related information;
- Manipulation — to include covert actions intended to control the behaviors of others;
- Pattern of Obstructive Behavior over Time — to indicate a cycle of negative behaviors directed at more than one person over a period of time;
- Ostracizes and/or Ignores Employees — to describe actions where the bully intentionally excludes, isolates, ignores, or "sidelines" an employee; and
- Gossips/Spread Rumors — to describe the act of spreading lies or rumors, or gossiping about certain individuals in an effort to discredit them.

Key Characteristics of a "Tough Boss"

As compared to their descriptions of workplace bullies, HR practitioners described "tough bosses" very differently, suggesting that their most prevalent characteristics include being:

- Objective and fair — reflecting the professional and objective judgment and decision-making of the manager;
- Self-controlled and unemotional — indicating that the manager's interactions at work are professional, unemotional, honest, consistent, and fair; and
- Results- and organizationally-oriented — indicating that the manager has high standards and holds employees accountable for meeting expectations, and consistently operates to achieve the best interests of the organization.

Positive Acts of a "Tough Boss"

As compared to a workplace bully, HR professionals identified the predominant work-related actions of a "tough boss" to be overwhelmingly *positive*, frequently including the following actions at work:

- Interactive, Two-Way Communication — reflecting the interaction and real listening and dialogue that occurs between the manager and his or her subordinates;
- Mentors and Tutors Subordinates — engaging in positive behaviors (for example, coaching, counseling, communication, and feedback) and using positive reinforcement in an effort to ensure that employees succeed; and
- Honest and Fair Conflict — indicating that the manager engages in healthy debate and discussion with others that is intended to resolve organizational issues.

Though exceptions undoubtedly exist, it initially appeared that a key distinction between a "tough boss" and a workplace bully might lie in their orientation toward work. Bullies are reportedly more *personally-focused*, meaning that they are often motivated at work by their own self-interest, and not the goals of the organization. Conversely, "tough bosses" are perceived to be more *organizationally-focused*, meaning that they are professional, objective, and fair-minded, have high standards, and hold employees accountable for meeting expectations, but consistently operate with the ultimate goal of achieving the best interests of the organization.

The Emergence of a New Conceptual Model

This distinction was, in fact, borne out by the study. However, in its most abstract form, this study resulted in the development of a new theory — expressed in the form of a conceptual model and noted in Figure 9.1.

Figure 9.1 Conceptual Model of Workplace Bully vs. "Tough Boss"

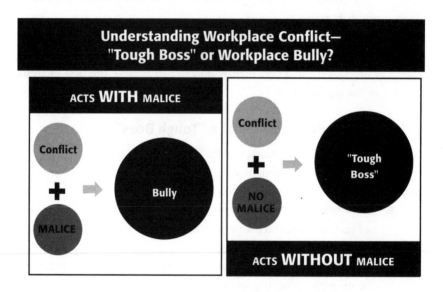

While incivility can be defined as "low-intensity, deviant behavior with ambiguous intent to harm the target and which violates the norms of respect,"[4] the results of this study suggest that workplace bullying is an unambiguous and *intentional* form of abusive behavior.

Workplace bullying is not "tough management," and the participants in this study were able to describe some very clear distinctions between the two types of managers. To the contrary, the results of this study suggest that a situation of workplace bullying can be determined by the presence or absence of *malice* — defined to mean "*the desire to cause pain, injury, or distress to another.*"[5]

A few representative comments of the study participants help to explain the *absence of malice* in the actions of a "tough boss":

- "I think the difference is that a tough boss is tough on everybody, not just one particular person. I think you can be tough, but at the same time not be a bully. You know, underneath the tough boss's character, I think you realize that he's just results-oriented to the point where it becomes like an obsession to him".

- "Fairness and intent differentiate a workplace bully from other conflicts. ... I didn't mind him saying (that's bull) because he respected me."
- "He may not be a great communicator, but his intent is considered by employees to be right."
- "There is a rational link between the pressures exerted by the boss to the performance required."
- "People understand that the boss has the "right intent" even when he or she is being tough on them."
- "No intent to intimidate, threaten or embarrass."
- "Good intentions geared toward making the company better."

On the other hand, the bullying manager who frequently humiliates a subordinate by criticizing their work in front of co-workers is, without a doubt, intending to cause the target some kind of pain. Representative comments from the participant interviews follow to show how participants discussed their perception of the bully's intentionality, and support the view that the *presence of malice* is a determining factor in deciding whether or not a situation is workplace bullying:

- "... with a bully, there's no goal orientation. There's nothing to do with your job. There's nothing to do with the company. ... It's simply something that has irritated the individual. It has maddened him to the point that they are driven to make a person's life miserable — as I said, either with verbal threats or actual actions against them. So, it's not like it's anything that, (gee, let's all work together on this.) It's just "this is mine. It strictly belongs to me, and I'm going to make you miserable. I am going to get you whatever it takes" and it's nothing to do with the job as much as it has to do with personal achievement with individuals. The person — it's an attack from one person to another, an all-out attack in some form or other."
- "... it was almost like she had to have a person to pick on and, at different times in the years that I was there, she would choose one person to direct her anger at, and she would do that for a year or so. Then she would pick on somebody else and leave that person alone.

Then the person was so relieved that she was leaving them alone that they almost became friendly with her."

- "Intentionally creates conflict with one (or a certain few) employees
- "Attempts to make others see the target as 'unworthy.'"
- "They take immoral, unethical, illegal, or physical actions that violate company policies."
- "I guess maybe throwing some of their weight or power [around] — like: 'I have the power to make you do something or make you feel like you need to do something.'"
- "Work to hide their manipulation and poor treatment of employees and co-workers."
- "Where a bully is concerned, they throw caution to the wind as far as feelings are concerned and their agenda is simply "I'm going to get you. I'm going to get this person. I'm going to make their life as miserable as I possibly can, and that's my goal in life."
- "Sets you up for failure and actually wants you to fail."
- "Vindictive and spiteful."
- "Ignores the well-being of fellow employees."
- "There is an intent to degrade employees."
- "Causes people to cry."
- "Creates an atmosphere of fear to get employees to react."
- "Browbeats employees."

Caution about the Use of the Study's Model

The proposed conceptual model is intended to assist HR professionals in making a critical distinction between workplace bullies and "tough bosses." It could be used by Human Resources to make an initial determination about whether or not the facts presented suggest that malice may be present. If so, this would serve as a signal to Human Resources that the next set of organizational protocols should be followed — moving from the target's subjective complaint to a more objective, fact-finding investigation by Human Resources. If the facts presented do not suggest that malice may be present, then HR could discuss with the complaining employee the reasons why the situation is not bullying (and not waste further time and organizational resources investigating the matter further).

It must be noted that it is not the role of Human Resources to determine guilt or innocence about a given workplace behavior. In administering policies, the role of HR might be seen as comparable to that of a grand jury in a legal setting — HR determines whether the evidence presented by the complaint warrants further action. The model developed, therefore, is not intended to create a "bright line" of distinction that would absolutely define a bully versus a "tough boss." It is only intended as framework for determining whether further HR and/or organizational action (e.g., investigation, discipline, etc.) should be taken.

Just as it occurs with complaints of sexual harassment, the same set of facts can be one or the other — either bullying or not. The determination depends on many factors, including the context of the interaction, the people involved, the frequency of the actions, the relationships between the parties, as well as the possible motives and intent of both individuals. In essence, determining whether or not bullying exists is not a mechanical process that can be solved with certainty or finality by a quick glance at the model. It is a professional HR determination (usually made in conjunction with management) that includes a comprehensive review of all of these issues in an attempt to make the most objective and fair decision possible. However, any determination is ultimately an interpretation of the facts and will, realistically, include some degree of subjectivity, despite the best efforts of everyone involved.

A difficult question arises for Human Resources when a situation involves "mixed motives" — meaning that while an individual may be motivated and work to meet organizational goals, he or she engages in bullying actions toward an employee based on personal animus. The results of this study suggest that if the individual frequently misuses power and authority, is personally-focused, is subject to frequent emotional outbursts, and engages in actions that are often perceived as unfair and inconsistent, then the aggregate result of these actions *suggest* that the presence of malice may exist and that further investigation by Human Resources is warranted.

Another thorny issue may arise if the results of an investigation are uncertain — that is, when Human Resources suspects that a problem may exist but the facts do not support a definitive conclusion. In other words, what happens if the answer at the end of an investigation is "maybe"? In such a situation, it might be advisable to (1) admonish the individual about proper workplace behavior, either through a friendly discussion or a more official verbal or written warning, depending on the facts generated during the investigation, (2) provide one-on-one coaching and closer supervision for a time (in order to better assess the possibility of a pattern of negative behavior), and/or (3) provide training to educate the individual about appropriate workplace behaviors and company policy, if applicable. However, the spectrum of possible interventions and responses to a complaint and investigation of bullying goes beyond the scope of this discussion.

It is important for HR professionals to be mindful that the use of the conceptual model (and any other types of screening tools) can inadvertently create a "false positive" or a "false negative." Simply stated, a false positive is any normal or expected behavior that is identified as anomalous or malicious. Alternatively, a false negative would be any abnormal or unexpected behavior that is improperly identified as appropriate such that no sanctions are applied.

Organizational policies for addressing a complex human problem like bullying cannot be adequately developed if they do not consider the possibility, however remote, of error. This author is not aware of any studies on bullying that have specifically focused on the topic of false accusations (perhaps due to a concern that such a focus would be perceived as one more example of "blaming the victim"). The fact remains, however, that there is a very real possibility that mistaken or false accusations of bullying may occur. As a result, it is incumbent upon Human Resources to be vigilant about ensuring the existence of a fair and equitable system for the resolution of interpersonal disputes at work.

Related Study Factors

The final category of discussion includes participant comments made in response to a number of specific questions that, while relevant, were only tangentially related to the study's central area of inquiry.

Personal Experience with Workplace Bullying

Part of the pre-interview screening process included asking the question "As an HR professional, have you ever had a personal experience with workplace bullying?" Eighty percent of the respondents indicated that they had personally experienced bullying at work. This was an unexpected result, given that HR professionals are the "internal police" in most organizations who have the duty to enforce policies, conduct training, mediate disputes, and ensure that employees are treated fairly. Of those who had experienced bullying on a personal basis, 100 percent reported that the bully was their immediate supervisor.

Given the recent incidence studies that have reported a bullying rate of roughly 34 percent of employees in the Southern part of the United States, an 80 percent prevalence rate in this study was very high and unexpected. What is it about Human Resources that is attracting this type of abusive treatment at work? This then begs the question: What needs to be done about it?

Length of Bullying Experience

The next subcategory of responses specifically addressed the issue of how long the participant had been in a given bullying situation. The average reported length of a bullying experience was 2.3 years (slightly over 26 months), with a cumulative total of 45.8 years of bullying experienced by the 20 participants in the study.

With an average reported duration of the abuse between 18-20 months, the length of exposure of HR professionals in this study was not consistent with earlier reports of bullying duration. This raises the obvious question: why would HR practitioners remain in these sorts of abusive work situations for such a lengthy period of time?

Organizational Adoption of an Anti-Bullying Policy

In response to the question "Does your organization have an anti-bullying policy?" only 35 percent reported that their organization had a written organizational policy that specifically prohibited workplace bullying. Could it be the absence of an anti-bullying policy that is contributing to the personal bullying that so many of them have experienced at work?

Possible Organizational Catalysts

Participants noted that there appear to be a number of organizational catalysts that interact to create a workplace climate where bullying can exist. These include the following:

- Employee frustration,
- Lack of training,
- Organization in chaos,
- Lack of comprehensive policies,
- Inadequate "checks and balances,"
- Misuse of power and authority,
- Poor management,
- Type of industry,
- Lack of communication,
- Times of change,
- Company culture,
- Conflict avoidance,
- Focus on "bottom line" at all costs,
- Managers with significant personal problems,

- Time pressures,
- Scarce resources (e.g., money/people),
- Union activity around contract time, and
- A "cover your butt" mentality.

Helpful HR Actions

In addition to identifying the organizational/system components that often lead to bullying behavior, participants also noted that, working closely with their legal counsel, Human Resources can make a huge difference in promoting a "culture of respect." These actions include:

- Zero-tolerance, starting with senior leaders;
- Clear expectations/accountability/consistency;
- Comprehensive policies;
- Code of conduct;
- Frequent employee communication;
- Disciplinary process;
- Promote a culture of trust and respect;
- Employee/manager training and coaching;
- 360-degree performance feedback;
- Establish multiple avenues of conflict resolution;
- 1-800 number with 24/7 access so that employees can report problems confidentially;
- Fair and thorough investigations;
- Quick action to resolve disputes;
- Periodic employee opinion surveys; and
- Conduct exit interviews with departing employees.

Potentially Positive Aspects of Workplace Bullying

Finally, the last question in this study was this: "Are there any positive benefits that workplace bullies provide to an organization?" Not surprisingly, eight of the 20 participants (40 percent) indicated that bullying is always "inappropriate" and could not identify any positive benefits that it might provide. Conversely, though, 12 of the 20 interviewees (60 percent) suggested that there may, in fact, be some positive benefits associated with workplace bullying.

Representative comments about the potentially positive impact of workplace bullying included the following:

- Employees sometimes band together — developing a warped sort of employee morale out of fear and distrust
- Makes HR more engaged with interacting with employees
- Because the bully won't take no for an answer, "he gets a lot of yess'es"
- We did things that we didn't think we could do — was that because of him or us?
- You know, I was able to do some stuff that I look back that I might not have had the guts to do if I wasn't a little bit afraid of him
- Employees learn to work around the bully
- Employees learn to do more on their own — they find answers some other way because they are afraid to approach the bully boss to ask questions
- Employee talents get recognized quicker because they have to work harder to get their job done
- People have to work harder to succeed in spite of the bully
- Initially, that focused "do what I say" does get results, but you can't sustain relationships in that type of situation
- Bullies can push employees for results and make them work harder
- If it does anything, it makes you go back and study HR policies and [that] made me better prepared to deal with the situation
- Made me thoroughly understand company policies
- More streamlined operations
- Did what we were told to do, but we were unhappy and turnover was high
- In the aftermath of the bully, it did bring the group together a bit
- More camaraderie [developed as a result of the co-workers rallying together]
- Felt less alone once I could talk openly about it
- To the individual who is the target, it will cause you to think ... and think hard ... about what you could have done to self-evaluate, and if you realize that there is something you could have done, you can take action to change it
- May make employees focus and work harder, but only for the short-term (if at all)

Although most of the participants responded that it was "a stretch" to find anything positive about this negative and abusive type of behavior, they were fairly consistent in their view that bullying had the effect of pulling their workgroup closer together as they rallied to each other's defense (but, as they noted, this camaraderie was not shown in the presence of the bullying manager). They also noted that bullying had the unintended effect of making them learn more on their own. Because they wanted to avoid interacting with the bully, they limited their "face time" with him or her as much as possible. Participants also suggested that bullying had a short-term effect of improving performance, as employees worked harder immediately following a bully's tirade.

The "So What" for HR Practitioners

Knowing how to identify workplace bullying has been a problem in the past due to a lack of clear definitions and very few descriptive research studies. From an applied standpoint, this conceptual framework provides an initial way to assess when a conflict-oriented situation is workplace bullying, and when it is simply a situation where a manager is operating as a "tough boss."

Once the possibility of bullying is initially identified, further investigation can take place to determine the appropriate organizational response. This new conceptual model will, hopefully, help you to make a quicker and more definitive determination about whether or not workplace bullying is taking place by assessing whether or not *malice* is present when dealing with a workplace conflict.

What HR Can (and Must) Do

// Businesses operate in their own self-interest — and it is in their interest to retain key employees and take action to stop bad managers from running off their talent.[1] //

The model outlined in Chapter 9 provides a way for you to make an initial assessment as to whether or not a conflict-oriented situation is workplace bullying. This chapter will help you identify those key areas that need your review in order to begin to proactively approach the issue of workplace bullying within your company.

Recommended HR Strategies

Taking a proactive approach to eliminate bullying from your organization will require a comprehensive review of the following components of your company's HR policies, practices, and procedures.

Review and Continuously Update Written Rules, Policies, and Agreements

It is important for employees to know what to expect so that they can anticipate how specific issues will be handled during the course of their employment. Communicating the company's expectations and "rules of the road" typically occurs through the distribution of an employee handbook and written policies, but may also be communicated during new-hire training or by written contracts and agreements to certain high-level individuals.

Employee Handbook. Employee handbooks are an excellent tool for compiling a company's key policies and rules into one manual that is typically distributed to each company employee at the time of initial hire. The handbook is generally set up in an easy-to-read form and is comprehensive in nature, typically covering important issues such as discrimination and harassment, expected business conduct, and the like.

It is fairly typical for a company to require each employee to sign an acknowledgment (which should be retained in the employee's personnel file) indicating that he or she has read the handbook and agrees to comply with its terms. This confirmation provides a paper trail confirming that each employee has been provided with a copy and has had an opportunity to review it and ask questions about it. It will also protect the company later should an employee attempt to claim that he or she was not aware of a company rule in order to escape discipline or as a defense in litigation.

HR Policies. Written policies are essential to provide guidance to a company's managers and employees about how certain issues should and will be handled. There should be clearly written policies that expressly prohibit harassment and discrimination, hostile work environment, employee abuse, and other key areas of concern for your company.

Agreements and Contracts. In addition to policies and handbooks, companies may also elect to enter into an employment agreement with certain key executives to ensure a common understanding about the employment relationship from the outset of the executive's employment. Companies may also want to include a provision that commits the executive to binding arbitration (rather than expensive litigation) to resolve any future employment-related disputes.

Maintain a Strong Management Team

Strong management teams are a key tool in a company's offense against high turnover and low employee morale. Senior leaders need to clearly understand their roles and what is expected of them. When they do, they are better able to do their job and can quickly correct poor performance or actions that are not consistent with the company's rules, goals, or philosophies.

Hire the Right People

A key strategy for reducing problems of bullying involves careful attention to your hiring process. Preventive measures include good interviewing skills and pre-employment screening (including a drug screen and background investigation that covers education, prior work history, any criminal background, plus a driver's license check).

While it is critically important to hire people with the right kind of experience and education, it is just as important to hire people who are a "good fit" for the organization. The way a company operates can have a significant impact on whether or not a certain type of candidate will be successful within that environment. As a result, hiring for "fit" should be a central part of the recruiting process.

New-Hire Orientation

Newly hired employees need to be trained about the company's key policies and rules, organizational structure, chain-of-command, business philosophy, expectations, and company culture ("how we do things around here"). This is important so that employees do not inadvertently "cross a line" that they did not even know existed. Some companies require employees to participate in orientation training even before they can begin their first full day of work in their assigned department.

In addition to this initial training, many companies match the new hire with a more seasoned employee who is the new employee's designated "mentor" for a specified time period (generally the first year of employment). The mentor is the new employee's "go to" person in the company — it is with the mentor that the new employee can ask questions, learn about how the politics and relationships work inside the company, and generally learn their way around the organization. If the new hire is lucky, the mentor will become a longer-term friend and ally over the course of the mentoring assignment.

Implement a Fair Grievance Process

Implementing a system through which parties can resolve conflict inside their company creates incentives for employees to consider resolving grievances with their employer, rather than engaging in costly and time-consuming litigation. The development of a grievance system not only diminishes costs for the organization,[2] but it also improves the morale of employees when they feel there are alternatives they can pursue to resolve conflicts and problems at work.

From least costly and quickest to most costly and most time-consuming, following are various alternative dispute resolution (ADR) methods that companies throughout the United States are currently using with successful results:

1. *Open-Door Policies.* These are policies that encourage employees to meet with their immediate supervisor to discuss and resolve work-related issues. It is a first step. For effectiveness, the company must: (a) indicate in its policies that there will be no negative repercussions when a complaint is voiced by an employee; and (b) provide ongoing training to managers about company policies, negotiation, mediation, and problem-solving.

2. *Senior Management Review.* The next step following the failure

of conflict resolution with the employee's immediate supervisor via the open-door technique is to have the issue reviewed by the next higher level of the management chain. This type of review gives the employee the ability to go up the hierarchy one level (or more) to the next most senior manager.

3. *Peer Review.* The aggrieved employee is given the opportunity to present his side of a dispute to a small panel of employees and supervisors selected from a pool of employees trained in dispute resolution. The method is often successful because employees participate in the decisions that affect them, breaking down barriers between management and employees. Though policies and rules differ by organization, peer review can be made binding on both parties (or not). If it is not binding and the resolution is not satisfactory to the employee, the dispute can be submitted to mediation or arbitration.

4. *Facilitation.* Facilitation provides an opportunity for a neutral employee within the organization to help resolve the dispute. Often the individual is an employee relations manager who acts as the key facilitator. The facilitator does not make judgments on the merits of disputes, nor does he or she provide a final decision. Rather, he or she helps both sides decide the best way to settle the dispute.

5. *Ombudsperson.* This is an individual who generally reports to a member of the company's senior management. The "ombuds" (as these roles are typically referred to) can be a full-time employee or an individual outside of the organization with whom the company contracts to provide this independent investigation and mediation service. Any conversation between an ombudsperson and an employee is held confidential. The ombuds can provide general information to management to help the company resolve the problem, but cannot divulge specific information provided by employees.

6. *Mediation.* This method requires the use of a mediator who is a neutral third party guiding two conflicting parties in exploring innovative solutions to their dispute. Mediators can be internal employees trained in conflict management and mediation or trained external mediators who have no perceived conflict of interest with the company. The willingness to resolve a dispute through mediation should be voluntary.

7. *Arbitration.* Arbitration is typically the most formal and costly, and frequently the most time-consuming, of all ADR alternatives. It is a formal process similar in nature to a court situation where an arbitrator issues a binding decision. In arbitration, witnesses may be presented and cross-examined. One advantage to a company in arbitration is that once a decision is rendered, there is finality, as there is not an appeals process governed by the Federal Arbitration Act.[3]

Conduct Regular Preventive Training

The trend in the courts and with governing federal agencies is an expectation that employers should provide regular compliance training for both managers and employees. Adequate, effective, and regularly scheduled employment law and practices training is now the rule — not the exception.

At a minimum, such training should provide a review of basic employment laws (for example, ADA, EEO, ADEA, OWBPA, FMLA, WARN, FLSA, etc.);[4] company rules, policies, and ethical guidelines; EEO practices in recruiting, hiring, training and development, compensation and benefits, succession planning, and promotion; harassment and discrimination; principles of negligent hiring, training, supervision, and retention; plus torts such as invasion of privacy and defamation.

The right training by professional and experienced trainers emphasizes building and maintaining a culture of success based on doing what is right — as opposed to a culture of minimal compliance and "just getting by."

Supervisors and managers are the key link between employees and their company. If these relationships are strong, then employees are more likely to be satisfied with their jobs and more productive as a result. Accordingly, it is very important to ensure that managers are properly trained in a number of key areas. These include:

1. *Communication.* Managers should receive training about how to communicate effectively with their staff. This is a critical skill on which all good relationships are built. Of key note, managers should know how to give complete and specific assignments, provide constructive feedback, respond to employee suggestions, and deal with conflict.

2. *Company Rules and Expectations.* Managers need to understand clearly what is expected of them, as well as fully understand the company's rules and policies. If the manager does not understand

his or her role in enforcing these rules, the result can be confusion and conflict. Companies often assume that managers understand their roles; however, it is more realistic to train managers so that true knowledge and understanding does exist.

3. *Work Assignments.* Managers should understand the strengths and weaknesses of their employees in order to determine what assignments are reasonable to give to each employee. Employees are at their most productive levels when they feel that their work is important and is valued by management. The key to finding this "sweet spot" in handing out work assignments is to train managers to assess the abilities of their employees so that they can assign work that is most compatible with each employee's strengths and weaknesses.

4. *Time Management.* Managers who manage time wisely are most respected by employees. If employees feel that their manager is "clueless" or does not utilize his or their time well at work, they are more likely to become cynical and less motivated.

5. *Conflict Resolution.* It is often the case that managers are so busy that they fail to notice problems that are occurring right under their noses. They are operating in a reactive, rather than a proactive, mode. Managers need to be trained to seek solutions, ask questions and set up systems to quickly solve problems before they turn into time-wasters and legal risks.

6. *Providing Performance Feedback.* It is essential for employees to be advised how they are doing in their jobs. Managers who constructively and frankly communicate this information to employees tend to establish stronger workgroups and better individual performers.

7. *Laws and Regulations.* It is crucial for managers to understand the basic laws and regulations that govern the employment relationship so that they have a general understanding of the rights of their employees. It is also necessary that they have enough knowledge that they can "spot" issues and seek counsel from a specialist in advance of responding to a problem. This ensures the fair treatment of their subordinates and also protects the company from being inadvertently exposed to potential legal issues as a result of their actions.

8. *Professionalism.* Managers who commit themselves to high

standards of professionalism and follow stringent business ethics gain the respect of their people. On the other hand, managers who "bend the rules" are viewed with skepticism. Employees will "walk through walls" for a manager who they believe will always do what is right — regardless of the political fallout.

Ensure Frequent Communication with Employees

Frequent, two-way communication will help to establish your company as one that truly values its employees by seeking to keep them informed. The most important and valued communications typically occur between employees and their immediate supervisors. This makes it even more important to ensure that your managers are trained not only to give a clear message, but also to actively listen. To ensure message consistency throughout your organization, consider providing your supervisors in advance with "talking points" or "highlights" to use when communicating with employees about sensitive company issues.

Other ways to ensure that you are proactively communicating with your employees include these methods:

1. *New-Hire Orientation.* Providing new hires with a thorough overview of your company's key policies, rules, and philosophies will go a long way toward starting your new employees off right. Understanding the company's culture and expectations will help employees have less stress, will help them become productive faster, and will also result in less initial turnover.

2. *Face-to-Face Meetings.* Having face-to-face meetings with people is considered to be the most "information-rich" and best way to give and receive information. This is because employees can ask for clarification and you can "read their body language" to ensure that true understanding of your message has taken place.

3. *Group Meetings.* Group and smaller staff meetings are a good way to provide information to employees, but they are not the best way to receive information back from employees. This is because many people do not feel comfortable sharing information in a group setting. So consider holding group meetings when you have a message that you want a large number of employees to hear, and host follow-up individual meetings if you want to get feedback and comments from employees.

4. *Newsletters.* While newsletters and postings are effective mediums

to communicate a consistent message to large groups of people, it would be a mistake to rely on these types of communication as your total communication plan.

5. *Employee Feedback.* It can be very useful to conduct periodic employee opinion surveys as a tool to forecast employee dissatisfaction that could lead to future problems. If employee feedback is solicited, though, employees need to be advised as to how it will be used so that they understand the process. What you most definitely don't want to happen is for employees to have unrealistic expectations about what, if anything, might change as a result of their input. This type of misunderstanding can create long-lasting damage to an organization.

Solid Performance Management and Feedback

The standard performance appraisal system of most companies consists of an employee filling out a performance review form independent of his or her manager. Then the two parties come together to discuss their ratings, as well as to discuss any differences in their assessment of the employee's results in meeting goals for the year. The performance review typically occurs on at least one occasion during the year (and some companies insist on quarterly or semi-annual reviews of performance). It is during this meeting that goals and objectives for the coming year are agreed upon.

A relatively new form of performance system is the 360-degree rating system. Under this approach, an individual solicits feedback about his or her performance from three primary sources: the manager, peers, and subordinates. By getting input from all of these different relationships, the goal is that the employee will receive a more thorough assessment of his strengths and weaknesses. This can be a particularly important strategy in getting the "accidental bully" focused on making adjustments to his or her behavior before it gets out of control.

Regardless of the system used, however, it is important for companies to implement some type of system that provides an opportunity for managers to give candid feedback to employees — and this feedback should be given not just at annual review time, but should occur frequently throughout the year. Without it, employees are left to wonder how they are doing and what their manager really thinks about them — which results in dissatisfaction, misunderstandings, and conflict over time.

Conduct Regular HR and Policy Audits

Most lawsuits can be traced to four distinct stages of the employment relationship:

1. Hiring (e.g., job descriptions, application forms, employment contracts, and references);
2. Employee evaluation (e.g., performance appraisals and promotions);
3. Employee discipline (e.g., rule infractions, evidence, and poor performance); or
4. Termination (e.g., comparison to other similar situations, proper warnings, complaint procedure followed, etc.).

As a result, it is important to audit these areas of your business on a regular and systematic basis to identify weaknesses or vulnerabilities in your systems. This will help you to identify issues that need to be updated — either to comply with new laws and regulations, to be consistent with best practices in your industry, or to upgrade them or simply make them more comprehensive.

Maintain a Designated Position(s) Focused Exclusively on Employee Relations

You can send a positive message to your workforce about the value your company places on maintaining positive employee relationships by establishing a position to exclusively handle employee relations matters. Most typically, these positions would reside within your Human Resources department.

The use of a company "ombudsperson" — an individual either inside the company or outside who has the responsibility to investigate and help resolve employee grievances — is a growing trend in the corporate world in recent years. Why? Because ombuds encourage and help facilitate an informal, early resolution of conflicts. The ombudsperson has a requirement to maintain employee confidentiality, so this encourages employees to come forward to attempt to resolve problems.

Another factor that may promote the growth of ombuds roles is the Sarbanes-Oxley Act of 2002.[5] This law encourages the reporting of corporate wrongdoing and prohibits retaliation against "whistleblowers." Since ombuds can alert management to whistleblowers' stories without naming their sources, possible retaliation is averted, likely resulting in more employees with concerns to come forward.

This confidentiality also can encourage employees to file complaints internally, which gives companies a chance to correct problems before they become full-blown nightmares. That is important because Sarbanes-Oxley does not require employees to file an in-house complaint before contacting an outside enforcement agency.

Ensure a Fair Termination Process

Most of us know from experience that the vast majority of litigation occurs when individuals feel that they were not "heard" or "taken seriously." Why? Because they feel like they were not given a fair chance. Implementing a system of progressive discipline is critical. Chances are that your employees will view your system as fair and equitable if you have provided employees with a fair chance to correct problematic behaviors before termination is considered. This perception of fairness will help to minimize emotions and disruptions by other employees on those occasions when an employee must be terminated from employment.

Systematic Follow-Up, Monitoring, and Implementation of Changes

Similar to your audit procedures, it is important to continually monitor your systems to ensure that they are up-to-date. It is also necessary to have follow-up mechanisms built into every one of them.

Consider designating someone on your staff (or an outside consultant) to monitor legal developments so that you can keep your HR policies and practices current. Likewise, it is important to keep track of your audit findings, hotline issues, employee survey results, and results of grievances filed and resolved so that you can identify trends in your employment-related issues. Identifying problematic issues, growth areas, or declining problem spots can help you to decide where to allocate your time, money, and preventive training resources. This will allow you to more strategically work on reducing employee problems in the future.

It is important to share survey findings and statistics regularly with your senior management team so that they understand developing workforce trends. To the extent that changes need to be made, encourage management to make the required decisions quickly. And do not forget to announce the changes to your employees — doing so will confirm to employees that your company takes these issues seriously.

Bullying and HR's Unique Organizational Role

There is no one in your company with the "standing" and organizational clout to deal with the issue of workplace bullying like you do as an HR professional. Even in the absence of a legislative requirement to do so, it is important for HR practitioners to explain to their senior management teams how expensive (in the long run) tolerating workplace bullying can be.

The need to focus management's attention on this issue is further supported by the results of the U.S. Workplace Bullying Survey (2007).[6] When informed about a bullying situation within their organization, American companies reportedly responded as follows:

- In 18 percent of the situations, the employer actually made the problem worse;
- In 44 percent of the reported bullying incidents, the employer either escalated the problem for the target or did nothing; and
- In only 32 percent of the situations did the employer help or try to assist in resolving the situation.

In sum, what this survey indicated was that in a full 62 percent of all bullying situations, employers either made the problem worse or *did nothing* whatsoever!

In addition, the survey also reported that in only 14 percent of the situations where a target sought help directly from Human Resources did the target actually receive assistance. Moreover, in 11.2 percent of the situations, HR reportedly sided with the bully-perpetrator. It is unclear how to evaluate this statistic without additional facts of the situations that were reported to Human Resources. However, the implication is that if HR uncritically supports management regardless of the situation, HR will be perceived by employees as part of the problem. HR cannot, and should not, be perceived as an ally for employees or managers who treat their subordinates or co-workers disrespectfully or, worse yet, abusively — regardless of their position or the perceived significance of their contribution to the company.

Dr. Gary Namie, widely regarded as a founder of and activist for the anti-bullying movement in the United States, succinctly covered the essence of what HR professionals and their companies must do to rid American corporations of managers who are abusive and disrespectful to their employees or co-workers, with this directive:

Don't play *"Whack-A-Mole."* It's useless and tiring. Instead, institute a policy that is faithfully enforced at all levels. No matter what rank the bully is, that person must face a challenge if the standards are violated.[7]

As more fully reported in Chapter 6, workplace bullying damages employee morale, affects productivity, creates turnover, results in more absenteeism, decreases job satisfaction, and increases stress-related medical costs — each reason enough for Human Resources to stand up and take action to eradicate this problem from the workplace. When employees feel valued and mutually respected, the interplay of that treatment often is translated into higher employee productivity and increased loyalty to the company.

HR's unique (and often difficult) role is to ensure a balance — that every employee is protected from abusive and bullying managers, *and* that managers have a right to insist on performance excellence and to hold employees accountable for meeting company objectives, even though they may be "tough." It is HR's job to understand the difference.

Responding to Workplace Bullying

// How about this? How about holding the abuser accountable? Gasp! What a concept![1] //

What does it take to build strong relationships between managers and employees based on fairness, trust, and mutual respect? You undoubtedly know the answer to that question — it takes time and energy (and an investment of money to conduct the necessary training and communications with employees that is required) to create this type of work environment. However, it is well worth the effort.

Think about it: *a culture of respect* (which takes its form as a positive employee relations climate) is the only type of environment that will — in the long run — lead to motivated, loyal, and high-performing employees focused on achieving the best results possible for their company. Conversely, *the climate of fear* created when bullying runs rampant most often results in decreases in employee morale and productivity; increases in absenteeism/sick leave, turnover, and litigation expenses; higher stress-related health costs; and increased workers' compensation claims and related costs.

Employees are critical resources, just as tools, materials, land, buildings, and financial investments of a company are also important resources. Without the employee talent necessary to implement a company's strategic plan, an organization will never meet its goals and objectives. However, there is a real risk that a constant focus on the "bottom line" at all costs may create an atmosphere where key supervisors and managers fail to nurture employee relationships or attend to employee issues with enough attention and care. The result: conflicts will escalate (or, when avoided, they will simply smolder — unresolved — under the surface), and a negative workplace climate may develop, leading to an increase in bullying and other forms of interpersonal conflict and/or abuse.

This chapter is designed to provide an overview of the strategies that have been recommended for confronting the bully, surviving as the target, responding from an organizational perspective, as well as looking at the issue from a systems viewpoint in order to obtain maximum leverage on the most critical factors that seem to yield a positive workplace climate where bullying is not tolerated.

Confronting the Bully

A number of anti-bullying activists strongly advocate that the only effective way to deal with bullies is to "stand up" to them. There are a number of books on the market today that are intended as "survival guides" for targets, and that provide information to help targets cope with bullies, as well as a series of tactics that individuals can use to fight back.[2]

Sam Horn suggests "28 ways to lose your bully," recommending the use of aggression as an approach to deal with a workplace bully. Given that verbal abuse is commonly used as a negative tactic by bullies, Horn encourages targets to become "*verbal samurais*" — to take command of the situation and stop the attack. According to Horn, targets need to be confident, courageous, wise, and proactive in order to rescue themselves. She also cautions that targets need to properly handle their anger, and be prepared financially and professionally.[3] The problem with a confrontational approach, though, is that there is generally a power differential between the bully and the target, making it difficult for the target to gain any leverage in such a situation.

Drs. Gary and Ruth Namie are advocates of a slightly less aggressive stance, recommending that targets think through the potential costs and impact of embarking on a legal fight or informal campaign to fight their bully. They are not proponents of using a company's internal grievance system, judging most as "not employee-friendly." Instead, they suggest a multi-dimensional strategy that they refer to as the "3 steps to topple tyrants."[4]

Their strategy includes the following informal campaign steps to confront the bully:

- Solicit support from family and friends;
- Consult a physician or therapist;
- Solicit witness statements from those who may have seen the bullying occur;
- Confront the bully;
- File an internal complaint;
- Prepare the case against the bully in terms of evidence, financial resources, and mental/emotional readiness;

- Present the case to senior managers, the internal tribunal, and other parties; and
- Take the case public.[5]

Although many authors have suggested taking legal action against bullies, bullying cases are rare and not often solved through legal channels in the United States. This is because current laws only protect targets when they are members of a "protected class" under Title VII of the Civil Rights Act of 1964. (See Chapter 7 for additional explanation about current laws and the proposed legislation that seeks to outlaw workplace bullying.)

Surviving as the Target

Self-Adjustment Strategies

Researchers and professional counselors have suggested a variety of strategies that individual targets can use to respond to workplace bullying. Harvey Hornstein refers to these efforts as the "change the victims" approach.[6] Suggested tactics under this approach involve limiting physical contact with the bully; emotion-focused therapy; self-adjustment; and accessing support from family, friends, the union (if present), colleagues, or the company's Employee Assistance Program (EAP). Others have suggested self-help survival strategies, including grieving, diverting attention to other parts of the target's life, the release of anger and anxiety in a peaceful way, being more optimistic through the use of humor, and working to rebuild self-esteem and move on.[7]

Drs. Gary and Ruth Namie, founders of the anti-bullying movement in the United States, suggest that family and friends are the first group of people that can help the targets of bullying — through their support, empathy, and the sharing of personal experiences.[8] Targets can also seek help from professional therapists, counseling services, employee unions, and legal services.

Though external support is obviously important, the Namies argue that the key step for targets is to become "bully-proof" to stop the hurt. Translated, what this actually means in terms of action required is that the target must assess the bully's impact, establish and protect individual boundaries, stop self-blaming, start controlling destructive emotions and anger, and affirmatively make requests about the satisfaction of his or her needs and wants.[9] To be sure, though, actually implementing these sorts of actions is easier said than done.

Emotional Intelligence Strategies

Other researchers have suggested an "emotional intelligence approach" for targets to deal with workplace bullies.[10] Since a key motivation of bullies is to see the pain of their targets, targets are encouraged to stay out of the bully's way and not allow them to see that their behavior is in any way intimidating to them. Targets are also encouraged to remain as calm and unperturbed as possible when under attack, and to try to identify the patterns of the aggressive behavior and avoid the bully during the times of outbursts. In addition, targets are encouraged to seek allies among colleagues and foster a relationship with a powerful mentor internally who can provide both political and emotional support.

Exit Strategies

In addition to the strategies focused on self-adjustment and emotional intelligence, as well as confrontation, a fourth approach suggested by some is to leave the job with dignity and seek new opportunities.[11] Often, the critical question for the target of workplace bullying is "should I stay and fight, or should I go?"

In 40 percent of all bullying cases, the target quits. And in another 24.2 percent of the cases, the target is terminated or driven out of the organization. That means that in more than 64 percent of all cases, the target leaves the organization, either voluntarily or through termination.[12] Given these fairly grim statistics, making an affirmative decision to leave the organization soon after it becomes apparent that the bullying is not going to cease is often in the target's long-term best interest.

Organizational Strategies to Consider

Organizations can (and, in my view, should) play a larger role in preventing and dealing with workplace bullying, particularly given that individual efforts of the target to end the conflict appear to be largely ineffective. Organization-wide initiatives are a necessary, and far more effective and lasting, way to deal with the issue of bullying. However, these possible actions are offered for your consideration only, as only you and your company (with advice from your legal counsel) can decide what actions and policies may be appropriate in your particular industry or environment.

Confront and Monitor Existing Bullies

To deal with existing bullying situations, some suggest that organizations must focus their attention on the abusive manager. The assumption is that bullies will change their abusive behavior with proper institutional monitoring and incentives.[13] It is recommended that achieving this type of individual change can best be accomplished in three key ways:

- Talking directly to the bully about the consequences of his or her behavior;
- Training bullies about how to treat others fairly in the workplace; and
- Implementing performance evaluation and appraisal mechanisms to discourage bullying behaviors, such as a 360-degree performance feedback system.

Senior Management Commitment to a Bully-Free Environment

In addition to confronting known bullies and advising them of the consequences of their behavior going forward, organizations need to demonstrate in visible and continuous ways that senior management is committed to addressing and eradicating the bullying phenomenon. Various studies have confirmed that the majority of employees who are bullied do not bring the issue to the attention of management.[14] Because of the power differential that typically exists in the relationship between the bully and the targeted employee, the reluctance to report bullying appears to be linked to the belief that nothing will be done and also to the fear of retaliation if something is done.

Organizations need to demonstrate enough will and credibility to fight against bullying through the implementation of a variety of concrete actions that support and work together to create a bully-free culture. These include:

- The development of an anti-bullying policy;
- The establishment of a policy implementation and monitoring mechanism;
- A system to investigate complaints and take immediate action to correct the situation, including the discipline and/or termination of the bullying manager;
- Training to set clear expectations about acceptable behavior at work and the consequences for failing to observe these expectations — at all levels; and
- A critical self-evaluation by Human Resources and the rest of

management about the respective past roles they have each played in dealing with this problem and how they might partner together in the future to eradicate the issue from the organization.

Each of these steps will be discussed separately as follows; however, before beginning to consider these options, it is important to note the following caveat:

You are strongly advised to seek legal counsel prior to beginning to consider the development of an anti-bullying policy and/or organizational strategy. This includes, but is not limited to, policy development, implementation and monitoring mechanisms, training, investigation and resolution procedures, employee communications, and/or any other forms of anti-bullying strategy implementation. Including legal counsel at the outset of any decision-making will ensure that your strategy will be structured in full consideration of applicable federal and state laws, governmental regulations, your company's policies, contractual issues, or any other relevant factors that might be uniquely specific to your company.

Anti-Bullying Policy Development

The development and implementation of a corporate anti-bullying policy is one of the first measures considered by companies seeking to create a culture that will not tolerate bullying.[15] If you decide to consider a policy, ideally an internal group (e.g., senior management, non-supervisory staff, union employees, Human Resources, etc.) should be formed to collaboratively address the issue and create the policy and action plan for achieving a bully-free workplace. The ownership and "buy-in" that occurs (as a result of an effort that incorporates the views of all major constituents) means the policy and action plan is more likely to be accepted than a policy created by an HR staff member working independently on the project, without much input.

A specific policy makes a clear statement of the organization's expectations about its culture and working relations among its employees. Basically, your policy will outline what type of behavior is acceptable, and what is not.[16] Culture really does matter, and behavior that is normatively deviant from your company's clear standards and expectations will be more quickly identified when there is a positive organizational culture in place.

Despite the fact that imitation reportedly provides an important impetus for the anti-bullying efforts of many companies,[17] any policy that you develop should be customized to fit your organization's specific culture, values, and needs. An anti-bullying policy will generally address the following types of issues: your company's commitment to a culture of mutual respect and zero-tolerance of bullying, clear definitions of bullying (what it is and what it is not), a list of behaviors that are not acceptable, examples of bullying situations, managerial responsibilities, the duties of HR staff, complaint procedures, any support or counseling offered to the target (e.g., EAP, etc.), training, assurances that all complaints are taken seriously and will be treated confidentially, a "no retaliation" provision, any appeal rights, and who to contact to get further information.

Despite the clear business case that confirms the reasons that we need to eliminate bullying from our organizations, it must be noted that only a handful of U.S. companies have publicly reported the implementation of a specific anti-bullying policy so far.[18] Companies for which policies have been confirmed are somewhat limited, but include Graniterock, Goodwill-Southern California, the Oregon Department of Transportation, and the Oregon Department of Environmental Quality (see the "Employer Policies" section of Chapter 7 for additional details about these specific policies).

For further guidance about developing your policy, see the sample anti-bullying policy included in the "Strategic HR Tools" located in Chapter 12.

Similarly, in the 2008 study of HR professionals discussed in Chapter 9, 35 percent reported that their organization currently had a written organizational policy that specifically prohibited workplace bullying.

The reason for the limited policy adoption (prior to a legislative mandate to do so) may stem from the fact that a number of management attorneys simply recommend updating the company's harassment policy to address "workplace bullying" without actually using those two words.[19] Essentially, what an organization would say is this:

Our policy is that all employees are entitled to a workplace
where you are not harassed for any reason.

The reason for this is concern that there is an argument to be made that a specific anti-bullying policy could potentially set employers up for a new employee cause of action. This is a result of the fact that courts are increasingly holding that written employment policies are enforceable as contractual agreements.

Policy Implementation, Enforcement, and Monitoring Systems

Whether or not you elect to develop and implement an anti-bullying policy, a specific internal group or department needs to be identified as being responsible for receiving complaints and educating your employees. Typically, this is the internal HR group in most organizations, but it does not have to be.

Monitoring the policy and the complaints received (and how they were resolved), as well as the periodic training delivered, is a necessary component of continuing to address whether or not the policy is effective. It also shows a continued commitment on behalf of your organization to the promotion of an atmosphere of zero-tolerance toward bullying.[20]

Investigation and Complaint Resolution Systems, Effective Disciplinary Procedures, and Follow-Up Measures

Finally, an investigation process is a necessary response to a bullying complaint (whether or not you elect to implement an anti-bullying policy). You can elect to use your internal resources, or you can contract with a third party external to your organization to provide this service. Regardless of which option you select, your organization will need to set clear ground rules that clarify how investigations will be conducted (and by whom), the confidentiality of the information (who can access notes, interviews, etc.), protections for the investigator, retention of relevant files, non-retaliation for reporting, and the like. And importantly, those responsible for conducting the investigation should be carefully trained so that they are perceived as credible and fair fact-finders by employees.

Following an investigation, you will need to consider all of the facts involved in the situation, make a decision, and then take action within a relatively short time frame. If the conflict has originated from personal issues, depression, stress, or deficiencies in conflict resolution or interpersonal skills, the issue may be solved relatively quickly through training, personal coaching, and/or individual therapy for the bully. Keep in mind that it is always possible that the individual accused of bullying may genuinely be unaware that his or her behavior is inappropriate, and a simple — but unambiguous — conversation may be sufficient to get his or her attention about the need to change the behavior.

For individuals who have taken abusive actions out of a desire to hurt others, it is imperative for Human Resources and the senior management team to be responsive to the early warning signals of bullying, assess the causes of the problem, and quickly and proactively intervene to resolve the situation in its earliest stages, if at all possible.

Importantly, all complaint resolution systems must include an effective disciplinary procedure that spells out the consequences for a failure to abide by the company's policy, including progressive discipline (typically verbal counseling, a written warning, suspension, and termination, usually in that order). It is important that you reserve your right to go straight to termination if the facts are egregious and dictate such a result.

Attention should be given to how you will communicate the results of your investigation when a complaint is ultimately resolved — not only with the affected individuals, but also their co-workers and other employees in your organization. Consider making a commitment to providing both parties with a detailed written response explaining the outcome of the investigation and the action to be taken. This will ensure that the decision has been made and that it is clearly spelled out for all concerned.

And lastly, it is reasonable to anticipate that at least some percentage of employees targeted by a bully will require assistance from mental health professionals, given the fact that 45 percent of all targets indicate that they experienced severe stress as a result of the bullying, often lasting more than a year.[21] This will depend, in large part, on the intensity and duration of the bullying. EAP counselors can be a valuable resource in restoring a target's confidence and mental health following such an episode.

Periodic Training about Conduct Expectations

Common sense, along with the work of several researchers in this field, suggests that enhancing the awareness of employees about bullying is a significant action that results in the prevention (or at least minimization) of its occurrence.[22] As a result, periodic training of employees must be conducted to ensure a culture of respect and accountability, and also that all employees understand the company's expectations about their workplace conduct — what *is* and *is not* acceptable — and the consequences for failing to observe these requirements.

If an organization does not frequently communicate its expectations about treating each other with respect, fairness, and dignity, bullies may mistakenly assume that abusive behavior toward others is an acceptable way to operate, or that "the ends justify the means." To the contrary, an organization must repeatedly encourage employees to raise their concerns, and confirm that all employee voices and opinions are valued, regardless of the rank of the employee.

Training on a regular basis, about treating each other with mutual respect, dignity, and fairness, will go a long way toward creating an organizational culture in which employees feel that they are trusted and respected, that their opinions and concerns are valued, that they have some degree of control over their worklife, and that there are opportunities for them to advance if they desire to do so. If such a change in the culture does not occur, bullying and other power abuses are likely to remain a problem.[23]

Common Management and HR Mistakes

When presented with a potential bullying conflict, management and HR, acting both together and separately, often make some common mistakes. These include:

- Not taking the conflict seriously or failing to deal with it in its early stages;
- Failing to realize that bullying is taking place (given that only 40 percent of all targets ever formally report the problem to management);[24]
- "Taking sides" with the alleged bully, as they are managers in 71 percent of all situations, and those in most decision-making positions are their colleagues;[25]
- Ignoring the problem because the bully is a strong performer; and
- Refusing to conduct an objective investigation because the target has been previously labeled as a "problem employee."

When we are alert to the most frequent response errors, we can be more vigilant about ensuring that our company does not make them in the future.

Critical Self-Evaluation by HR

As HR professionals, we cannot simply take the view that this is the bully's problem, or the company's problem. A key role of Human Resources is to protect both the company *and* its employees, making it our problem too. Among other things, we can be confident that workplace bullying raises health insurance costs, increases absenteeism, and reduces productivity and employee morale/loyalty. As a result, we must critically self-evaluate our attitudes and actions in order to really make a difference in eradicating the problem from our organizations.

Simply because there is no law requiring us to affirmatively deal with the problem of workplace bullying is no reason not to take steps to improve our overall workplace climate. Recent studies have indicated that organizational measures to counteract bullying are positively related to three factors:

- A company's adoption of "sophisticated" or "high-performance" HR practices (e.g., extensive training, the use of a formal performance appraisal, and regular employee attitude surveys),
- Previous negative publicity about bullying in the company's workplace, and
- The presence of a young HR manager.[26]

While you obviously cannot change your age, you *can* have a significant impact on the implementation of "high-performance" HR practices in your company. Sadly, researchers have also noted that a company's HR department is seldom portrayed as a center of support and advice for either the targets of bullying or for the bullying manager.[27]

While the exact costs and extent of bullying may not be easy to measure, issues such as turnover, absenteeism, and employee complaints are certainly quantifiable. Human Resources is generally the first group to become aware of departments with high turnover or repeated complaints from employees in a workgroup managed by a certain supervisor. As a result, it is important for HR to maintain detailed absence and turnover records (by department) in order to keep track of developing patterns. In addition, exit interviews should be conducted with departing employees in an effort to identify problematic managers that have not yet been publicly identified.

In addition to these steps, it must be noted that employees generally will not begin to trust that their organization is really serious about its new anti-bullying position until the first complaint under the new policy is resolved fairly and quickly. To this end, it is critical to ensure that the complaint investigation and resolution system includes appropriate procedures and timely resolution of the issues, and that the individuals responsible for managing the process are properly educated and professional in their approach.

Despite our sometimes smug view of our profession as one that listens to and actively assists employees in a variety of personal and professional matters, recent facts reveal a different story. The recent U.S. Workplace Bullying Survey (2007) results[28] suggest that bullies operate with confidence that they are not likely to be punished because they frequently enjoy support from higher-ranking company officials who can protect them if and when they are exposed. In fact, 43 percent of bullies reportedly have a high-ranking "executive sponsor." Another 33 percent thrive because of support received from their peers, mostly fellow managers, and 14 percent of all bullies receive assistance *from HR* (i.e., HR "sides" with the bully).

According to the same survey, 77 percent of targets lose their jobs to make the bullying stop, while bullies experience negative consequences in only 23 percent of the reported incidents.[29] In addition, when presented with a bullying situation, in 62 percent of all bullying situations, the employer reportedly either does nothing, or what it does do actually makes the situation worse![30]

It is possible that many of the reported situations actually might have been a result of legitimate, work-related conflict and not bullying. However, these statistics deserve a closer look, and possibly some difficult soul-searching for us all.

Some questions that you might ask of yourself and your organization:

- Have we adopted the kind of "high-performance" HR practices that will help to create a positive culture for our organization and its employees?
- Do employees seem reluctant to come to HR for help in resolving workplace conflict (e.g., how many complaints are investigated and resolved each month)?
- Does our group maintain monthly statistics related to turnover, absenteeism, workers' compensation claims, and the like? Do we *act* on the information contained in those reports?
- Is HR perceived as an ally of abusive managers, or as being so entrenched and aligned with senior management that it fails to objectively review these types of situations?
- Does HR conduct objective and fair investigations, or does it frequently end up with a result that is the safest and easiest conclusion for the organization?

As a result of recent statistics, it is clear that both HR and management need to take a self-critical inventory of their respective past roles in dealing with this issue (or failure to deal with the issue), and then work together to take the necessary actions to address this destructive workplace problem. If companies voluntarily act to take these proactive steps to end the problem, advocates for a legislative mandate would have a much weaker legal argument about the need for change.

Ironically, in the world of business, it sometimes seems as if managers who "mess up" are moved into ever higher positions of responsibility in the organization (to the shock and dismay of those who have worked with them most closely). If we are vigilant about requiring professionalism and respect at work, this type of situation will be the exception, instead of the rule it seems to be today. As Drs. Gary and Ruth Namie so aptly remind us, "Good employers purge bullies; bad ones promote them."[31]

Strategic HR Tools

II Until there's a public commitment, and action to back that commitment, a policy is only words on paper.[1] *II*

Every HR professional that I have ever known appreciates decision-making "tools" and checklists that help to get their job done, particularly given that most of us are usually strapped for both time and resources.

Here are some strategic tools that will, hopefully, help you to build a "culture of respect" where bullying and harassment are not tolerated. Included in this chapter are the following:

- Sample Survey of Employees and Managers — a survey that you can use to assess the extent of the problem of bullying within your company;
- "Culture of Respect" Climate Assessment — a "quick and dirty" inventory of your company's implementation of the most effective strategies that work together to create a positive employee relations climate;
- Developing a "Culture of Respect" Strategy: *Future Action and Planning* — a strategic planning tool to help you assess your company's "current state" against where you want to go;
- The "Brutal Boss" Questionnaire — a survey to help you determine whether or not you are working for a bully boss;
- Some Real-Life Examples: Case Studies and Key Insights — an overview of several real-life workplace examples of bullying, the outcome of each, as well as key insights about the learning that occurred as a result of the conflict;
- SHRM Sample Policy on Workplace Bullying — a model policy that you can use as a starting point for the development of your own anti-bullying policy; and

■ A Checklist for "Bully-Proofing" Your Organization — though not exhaustive, this checklist is a good start for beginning to think about the necessary actions you will need to take as you begin the process of promoting a "culture of respect" within your organization.

Sample Survey of Employees and Managers

All of the information that you provide in this survey or in further conversations will be kept completely confidential, and your name and/or company will never be identified if you elect to participate in this or further studies. Many thanks for your participation!

Your Direct Experience of Bullying

1. Have you ever been bullied at work?
❑ Yes ❑ No (if your answer is No, please skip to Question 8)

2. Who bullied you?
❑ Your immediate supervisor
❑ Colleague
❑ Other manager
❑ Member of your company's senior management team
❑ A direct report to you (subordinate)

3. What form(s) did the bullying take?
❑ Unfair criticism
❑ Intimidating behavior
❑ Opinions ignored
❑ Humiliation and/or ridicule
❑ Verbal abuse
❑ Malicious lies or accusations
❑ Excessive monitoring
❑ Information withheld
❑ Responsibilities taken away
❑ Unreasonable workload or goals
❑ Decisions arbitrarily overruled
❑ Exclusion from meetings
❑ Training withheld

❑ Refused leave or time off
❑ Promotion blocked
❑ Exclusion from social events
❑ Physical abuse

4. What, in your view, was the primary reason that you were targeted for the bullying?
❑ Personality clash
❑ Gender
❑ Age
❑ Race
❑ Part-time status
❑ Sexual orientation
❑ Temporary contract status
❑ Disability
❑ Religious beliefs
❑ Other (Please describe:

_____)

5. How long did the bullying last or has the bullying been going on?
❑ Under 1 month
❑ 1–3 months
❑ 4–6 months
❑ 7–12 months
❑ Over a year

6. How did the bullying affect you?

❑ Made me worry about coming to work

❑ Affected my confidence

❑ Affected my self-esteem

❑ Affected my sleep

❑ I became depressed

❑ Affected my health

❑ I became irritable

❑ Anxiety and panic attacks

❑ Affected the quality of my life

❑ I had to take time off work

❑ Increased alcohol/tobacco consumption

❑ Other (Please describe:

_____)

7. What action(s) did you take to try to stop the bullying?

❑ Talked with family and/or friends

❑ Talked with colleagues

❑ Started looking for another job

❑ Saw a doctor

❑ Spoke with a senior manager

❑ Spoke with HR

❑ Made an informal complaint

❑ Spoke with my immediate manager

❑ Sought legal advice

❑ Contacted an external agency

❑ Other (Please describe:

_____)

8. Did any of those actions positively help to deal with the problem?

❑ Yes

❑ No

❑ In part

❑ Made the situation worse

Your Indirect Experience of Bullying

9. Have you ever witnessed colleagues in your own department being bullied?

❑ Yes ❑ No

10. Are you aware of bullying occurring elsewhere in your organization?

❑ Yes ❑ No

11. What form(s) did the bullying take?

❑ Unfair criticism

❑ Intimidating behavior

❑ Opinions ignored

❑ Humiliation and/or ridicule

❑ Verbal abuse

❑ Malicious lies or accusations

❑ Excessive monitoring

❑ Information withheld

❑ Responsibilities taken away

❑ Unreasonable workload or goals

❑ Decisions arbitrarily overruled

❑ Exclusion from meetings

❑ Training withheld

❑ Refused leave or time off

❑ Promotion blocked

❑ Exclusion from social events

❑ Physical abuse

12. What, in your view, was the primary reason for the bullying?
- ❏ Personality clash
- ❏ Gender
- ❏ Age
- ❏ Race
- ❏ Part-time status
- ❏ Sexual orientation
- ❏ Temporary contract status
- ❏ Disability
- ❏ Religious beliefs
- ❏ Other (Please describe: _____

_____

_____)

13. What actions are you considering to stop workplace bullying in your department or workgroup?

_____

_____

_____

_____

_____

_____

14. What actions do you think our company should consider implementing in order to stop workplace bullying, if any?

_____

_____

_____

_____

_____

_____

"Culture of Respect" Climate Assessment

Please review the list below, and check off each of the following HR/ employee relations tools currently utilized by your company. Calculate the total number of tools that are currently in use, and then check your results against the scale below.

___ Written Rules, Policies, and Agreements

___ Strong Management

___ Hire the Right People

___ A Fair Grievance Process

___ Preventive Training for Managers and Employees

___ Frequent and Honest Employee Communications

___ Comprehensive Employee Benefit Programs

___ Performance Management and Feedback System

___ Regular Audits of Your Policies and Employment Practices

___ Designated Employee Relations Positions

___ A Fair Termination Process

___ Systematic Follow-Up, Monitoring, and Implementation of Changes

___ TOTAL POINTS

SCALE

0–3 You've Got Some Work to Do

4–6 Some Progress/Consider Adding More Tools — Mildly Positive

6–9 You've Implemented Many of the Right Tools — Moderately Positive

9+ Congratulations! Full Range of Tools in Place — Very Positive

Developing a "Culture of Respect" Strategy:
Future Action and Planning

1. Written Rules, Policies, and Agreements

WHAT WE DO NOW:

_____

_____

_____

_____

WHAT WE SHOULD CONSIDER:

_____

_____

_____

_____

2. Strong Management

WHAT WE DO NOW:

_____

_____

_____

_____

WHAT WE SHOULD CONSIDER:

_____

_____

_____

_____

3. Hire the Right People
WHAT WE DO NOW:

_____

_____

_____

_____

WHAT WE SHOULD CONSIDER:

_____

_____

_____

_____

4. A Fair Grievance Process
WHAT WE DO NOW:

_____

_____

_____

_____

WHAT WE SHOULD CONSIDER:

_____

_____

_____

_____

5. Preventive Training for Managers and Employees
WHAT WE DO NOW:

_____

_____

_____

_____

WHAT WE SHOULD CONSIDER:

_____

_____

_____

_____

6. Frequent and Honest Employee Communications
WHAT WE DO NOW:

_____

_____

_____

_____

WHAT WE SHOULD CONSIDER:

_____

_____

_____

_____

7. Comprehensive Employee Benefits Program
WHAT WE DO NOW:

_____

_____

_____

_____

WHAT WE SHOULD CONSIDER:

_____

_____

_____

_____

8. Performance Management and Feedback System
WHAT WE DO NOW:

_____

_____

_____

_____

WHAT WE SHOULD CONSIDER:

_____

_____

_____

_____

9. Regular Audits of Your Policies and Employment Practices
WHAT WE DO NOW:

_____

_____

_____

_____

WHAT WE SHOULD CONSIDER:

_____

_____

_____

_____

10. Designated Employee Relations Positions
WHAT WE DO NOW:

_____

_____

_____

_____

WHAT WE SHOULD CONSIDER:

_____

_____

_____

_____

11. A Fair Termination Process
WHAT WE DO NOW:

_____

_____

_____

_____

WHAT WE SHOULD CONSIDER:

_____

_____

_____

_____

12. Systematic Follow-Up, Monitoring, and Implementation of Changes
WHAT WE DO NOW:

_____

_____

_____

_____

WHAT WE SHOULD CONSIDER:

_____

_____

_____

_____

The "Brutal Boss" Questionnaire

For an assessment of your current experience of abuse by superior(s) and its possible consequences for your health, well-being, and work productivity, complete the questionnaire that follows. Then find your personal rating using the scoring information that is provided on the reverse side.

Rate your boss on the following behaviors and actions. If you agree that a statement categorizes your boss, write a number from 5 to 8, depending on the extent of your agreement. If you disagree with a statement in reference to your boss, write a number from 1 to 4, depending on the extent of your disagreement.

1 2 3 4 5 6 7 8
1 = Strongly disagree 8 = Strongly agree

1. My boss deliberately provides me with false or misleading information. ___
2. My boss treats me unfairly at times for no apparent reason. ___
3. My boss deceives me sometimes. ___
4. My boss deliberately withholds information from me that I need to perform my job. ___
5. My boss criticizes low-quality work from me. ___
6. My boss tells me how I should be spending my time when not at work.
   ___
7. My boss will "get" me if I don't comply with her/his wishes. ___
8. My boss humiliates me in public. ___
9. My boss calls me unflattering names. ___
10. My boss requires that her/his standards be met before giving a compliment. ___
11. My boss believes that I am generally inferior, and blames me whenever something goes wrong. ___
12. My boss acts as if s/he can do as s/he pleases to me, because s/he is the boss. ___
13. My boss treats me like a servant. ___
14. My boss expects me to dress appropriately at all times. ___
15. My boss treats me unjustly. ___
16. My boss steals my good ideas or work products and takes credit for them.
    ___
17. My boss will make me "pay" if I don't carry out her/his demands. ___

18. My boss displays anger publicly toward me by shouting, cursing, and/or slamming objects. ___
19. My boss criticizes me on a personal level rather than criticizing my work. ___
20. My boss demands that I give my best effort all the time. ___
21. My boss is tougher on some subordinates because s/he dislikes them regardless of their work. ___
22. My boss is discourteous toward me. ___
23. My boss is dishonest with me. ___
24. My boss shows no regard for my opinions. ___
25. My boss is deliberately rude to me. ___
26. My boss lies to me. ___
27. My boss misleads me for her/his own benefit. ___
28. My boss insists that I work hard. ___
29. My boss displaces blame for her/his own failures onto me. ___
30. My boss openly degrades and/or personally attacks me. ___
31. My boss mistreats me because of my lifestyle. ___
32. My boss demands that I constantly do high-quality work. ___
33. My boss reprimands me in front of others. ___
34. My boss deliberately makes me feel inferior. ___
35. My boss is not honest with the people who rank beneath her/him. ___
36. My boss threatens me in order to get what s/he wants. ___

Scoring

Total your responses to the following questions:

\# 5 ___

\# 10 ___

\# 14 ___

\# 20 ___

\# 28 ___

\# 32 ___

"Tough Boss" total: ___

Now total your responses to the remaining 30 questions.

"Bad Boss" total: ___

KEY

Tough boss total + bad boss total = Assessment of boss

Under 36 + Less than 90 = Not particularly tough.

36 to 48 + Less than 90 = Tough, but not abusive.

36 to 48 + 90 to 195 = Tough, with instances of abuse. Adverse effects on work and well-being may very well occur.

Any Over 195 = Abusive. Deteriorating mental and physical health and lowered productivity are associated with this level of mistreatment.

Source: "The Brutal Boss Questionnaire," from Brutal Bosses and Their Prey *by Harvey A. Hornstein, copyright © 1996 by Harvey A. Hornstein. Used by permission of Riverhead Books, an imprint of Penguin Group (USA) Inc.*

Some Real-Life Bullying Examples: Case Studies and Key Insights

Mr. C — Subsidiary CEO of A Corporation

Mr. C was an ambitious professional in charge of a subsidiary unit of a large corporation. Since he worked in a separate building, he had a great deal of flexibility and not much visibility to senior management. He operated pretty much as he pleased, with no one the wiser.

He had a reputation as one who played favorites with his staff. He was also known for his angry and unpredictable outbursts in the office. His employees feared him, but they worked hard to stay out of the "line of fire" and not make him angry.

An anonymous report tipped the company off that Mr. C was harassing and intimidating several employees on his staff, all of whom happened to be female. An investigation was commenced, and all members of the staff were interviewed, including Mr. C and his top management personnel. As a result of the investigation and subsequent recommendations, Mr. C's employment was terminated by the subsidiary's Board of Directors.

On the day he left the organization, the company's chief investigator received a bouquet of a dozen yellow roses at his office at work. The card read simply: "Although we were yellow (cowardly), you showed great courage. Our thanks and admiration, The Girls."

Key Insight: *Standing down a bully is easier if you have corporate policy and senior management on your side.*

Mr. Z — Senior Vice President, Corporate, of B Corporation

Mr. Z, a senior officer with responsibility for a department about to undergo a cost-cutting review and significant reorganization, was not at all happy about the review. After several weeks of independent reviewers asking for information and scrutinizing his budget, numerous budget areas were identified and suggested for elimination.

One day after lunch (and the timing is important), he called the company's internal legal counsel, Jeff, to discuss the project. He suggested that Jeff should discontinue his work immediately. Jeff wisely told him that he could not suspend his work, given that he had been assigned to the project by the company's senior management team. Not one to mince words, Mr. Z then unwisely said to Jeff something like this: "If you don't back off, I will run you over like a Mack truck."

Jeff reported the incident to his department head and was told: "Don't worry about it. He has had a drinking problem for a long time and was probably drunk when he called you." Later, a member of the company's senior management team called to tell him that he was "doing a great job and to please continue — you are obviously getting somewhere, given his strong resistance." Mr. Z's employment with the company was later terminated for a variety of reasons, but due in large part to this bullying incident and many others like it.

Key Insight: *Bullies may protest and bluster, but even high-level bullies can be stopped with a direct approach and a refusal to back down (and, most importantly, senior management support)!*

Mr. Q — Senior Vice President & General Counsel of C Corporation

After reporting to Mr. Q for several months, Marcia began to get calls from employees about her boss, complaining about his aggressive and bullying-type interactions with others and his heavy-handed decision-making style, and making allegations about an inappropriate personal relationship with his secretary. After some time, she decided that she could no longer "provide cover" for him within the company nor could she continue to explain away his behavior. She disagreed with his approach and decided — somewhat emphatically — that she no longer wanted to be associated with him as a colleague.

Marcia requested a transfer to another part of the organization, but her senior management advised that they wanted her to continue to be part of this new company to "keep an eye" on things. She resigned two weeks to the day after her transfer request was rejected. The senior management team just did not believe that she would really walk away, given her loyalty and long service to the company.

The company's Chief Executive Officer called and requested that Marcia make time for a private meeting. He asked her to stay and offered to change her reporting relationship. While appreciative of the gesture, she told him that she was "already well past ready to leave" such a toxic environment. She asked the CEO to "take a long, hard look" at Mr. Q's overbearing actions, given her view that his behavior was "poisoning the company."

Mr. Q's employment was terminated by the company within one year of Marcia's departure.

Key Insight: *If you can't fix a conflict situation with your supervisor somewhat quickly (regardless of rank, but especially true when that person is a "power broker" within the organization), sometimes it is better to leave a bad work situation than to continue to allow a toxic boss to permeate your professional and personal life.*

Mr. D — Vice President & Chief Operating Officer of D Corporation

Mr. D was an egocentric man with self-confidence that was out of proportion (in Joe's humble opinion) to his actual skill level. After several months of working together well after Joe started working for the company, Mr. D began to send Joe email notes that were in all-caps and on which he copied many extraneous people. Several people also complained to Joe (as he was the VP-Human Resources) that Mr. D's behavior with his immediate workgroup was intimidating to his staff and that most were very much afraid of him.

Joe called Mr. D and requested that they get together to talk about why Mr. D. was being so hostile to him and others in the company. He said, "What are you talking about?" The notes stopped, and he never would agree to set a time to actually meet with Joe to discuss the problem, but it never occurred (at least to Joe's knowledge) again.

As a company executive, Mr. D was required to participate in a 360-degree performance feedback review where his boss, peers, and subordinates all commented on his performance and behavior. Then he was required to spend several months working with an outside executive coach one-on-one to help develop his people skills. Despite the company's best efforts, Mr. D's employment was terminated by the company within the year.

Key Insight: *Direct confrontation with bullies often works to resolve the problem (or at least encourages the bully to find someone else to abuse). Bullies are generally the aggressors in a conflict situation, but tend to shy away from confrontational situations that they themselves do not initiate and over which they do not retain control.*

Mr. L — Vice President of E Corporation

Mr. L worked for a small private company that grew very quickly through a series of mergers and acquisitions. He had only a high-school education, but was viewed as a "trusted key guy" by the company's owner. He was definitely in over his head. Stephen was hired to help the company professionalize its legal and HR practices because they did not have an experienced internal staff.

Within two months, Stephen identified the first problem: the company did not pay its non-exempt employees overtime pay for time worked in excess of 40 hours per week. When he advised Mr. L that this was a problem, he told him, "Don't worry about it — we give our employees turkeys at Thanksgiving and hats at Christmas." He explained that the Fair Labor Standards Act was the law and did not allow for turkey and hat exceptions in lieu of overtime pay.

Within two weeks, the company approached Stephen and asked to buy out the balance of his three-year contract. It was only then that he understood that, to them, it would be cheaper to buy out his contract than to actually fix the problem. With Stephen gone, there would be no one else internally who would push the issue.

Stephen reluctantly left his position with the company; however, his employment contract was litigated and he refused to settle until he received assurances from the company's lawyers that they would observe their overtime obligations to the company's employees. It was a difficult time in Stephen's life. Although accepting the buyout would have been easier for him personally, he felt it would have been unethical to walk away while the company's employees continued to be paid unfairly and in violation of the law.

> **Key Insight:** *As a person in HR with a strong sense of ethics, Stephen felt that he had a responsibility to the employees to make sure that they were treated legally and fairly. Once he was informed that the company had fixed its pay practices such that overtime would be paid going forward, he agreed to accept the settlement of her contract terms. Sometimes, in responding to a bully, the underlying good character of those involved in resolving the problem has an opportunity to shine.*

Lessons Learned from These Real-World Examples

So, what can we take away from these real-world encounters and their outcomes? In my view, the predominant lesson is that *early and direct action* is the best strategy for diffusing conflict situations with difficult people. As a result of my own experience, research, and observation, I have come to believe that it is critical to "stand down" a bully through assertive and unequivocal action. Once a bully understands that his target will not silently "take it," he will usually back off in search of easier "prey."

Bullies are usually focused on the misuse of their power and control, frequently operating in their own personal interest rather than for the good of the organization. As a result, if they discover that they cannot completely dictate the terms of an encounter, or if they sense resistance that could prove to be problematic for them personally, they often choose not to continue to engage in a conflict that they think they might lose.

SHRM Sample Policy on Workplace Bullying[2]

[Company Name] defines bullying as *"repeated inappropriate behavior, either direct or indirect, whether verbal, physical or otherwise, conducted by one or more persons against another or others, at the place of work and/or in the course of employment."* Such behavior violates [Company Name] Code of Ethics, which clearly states that all employees will be treated with dignity and respect.

The purpose of this policy is to communicate to all employees, including supervisors, managers and executives that [Company Name] will not *in any instance* tolerate bullying behavior. Employees found in violation of this policy will be disciplined, up to and including termination.

Bullying may be intentional or unintentional. However, it must be noted that where an allegation of bullying is made, the intention of the alleged bully is irrelevant, and will not be given consideration when meting out discipline. As in sexual harassment, it is the effect of the behavior upon the individual that is important. [Company Name] considers the following types of behavior examples of bullying:

- Verbal Bullying: slandering, ridiculing or maligning a person or his or her family; persistent name-calling which is hurtful, insulting or humiliating; using a person as the butt of jokes; abusive and offensive remarks
- Physical Bullying: pushing; shoving; kicking; poking; tripping; assault, or threat of physical assault; damage to a person's work area or property
- Gesture Bullying: non-verbal threatening gestures, glances that can convey threatening messages
- Exclusion: socially or physically excluding or disregarding a person in work-related activities

In addition, the following examples may constitute or contribute to evidence of bullying in the workplace:

- Persistent singling out of one person
- Shouting, raising voice at an individual in public and/or in private
- Using verbal or obscene gestures

- Not allowing the person to speak or express himself or herself (i.e., ignoring or interrupting)
- Personal insults and use of offensive nicknames
- Public humiliation in any form
- Constant criticism on matters unrelated or minimally related to the person's job performance or description
- Ignoring/interrupting an individual at meetings
- Public reprimands
- Repeatedly accusing someone of errors that cannot be documented
- Deliberately interfering with mail and other communications
- Spreading rumors and gossip regarding individuals
- Encouraging others to disregard a supervisor's instructions
- Manipulating the ability of someone to do their work (e.g., overloading, underloading, withholding information, setting meaningless tasks, setting deadlines that cannot be met, giving deliberately ambiguous instructions)
- Inflicting menial tasks not in keeping with the normal responsibilities of the job
- Taking credit for another person's ideas
- Refusing reasonable requests for leave in the absence of work-related reasons not to grant leave
- Deliberately excluding an individual or isolating them from work-related activities (meetings, etc.)
- Unwanted physical contact, physical abuse or threats of abuse to an individual or an individual's property (defacing or marking up property)

See also: SHRM Sample Policy on Investigating Workplace Conduct[3] and SHRM Sample Policy on Sexual and Other Unlawful Harassment.[4]

(Reprinted with permission from the Society for Human Resource Management.)

A Checklist for "Bully-Proofing" Your Organization

Organizational Culture
❑ Create a zero-tolerance culture that does not tolerate bullying/harassment
❑ Educate management about the issues and make sure you have their commitment
❑ Encourage an open-door policy among managers

Employee Communication
❑ Communicate to employees and managers regularly about the company's values and expectations that employees at all levels are to be treated with respect and fairness
❑ Clearly communicate to employees and managers about acceptable forms of behavior and the consequences of failing to observe these expectations (use examples)

Training for Managers and Employees
❑ Conduct training regularly for managers and employees about how to deal with and resolve conflict

Policy Development
IF YES to NEW POLICY:
❑ Set up a strategic team to work together on the development of the new policy
❑ Develop and communicate the new anti-bullying policy to all employees
❑ Identify the group or individual who will have the primary responsibility to monitor the policy and investigate claims
❑ Create a system (with clear procedures) to investigate and resolve complaints
❑ Make sure the investigators are well-trained so that they can conduct investigations fairly and can respond quickly
❑ Conduct training for employees and managers about acceptable forms of behavior and the consequences of failing to observe these expectations

IF NO to NEW POLICY:

❏ If you decide *not* to adopt a new policy, consider making changes to your current harassment policy so that it covers all forms of harassment at work (including bullying and other forms of intentional abuse)

❏ Investigate and resolve bullying complaints promptly, using a fair investigation and resolution system

❏ Regularly encourage employees to report conflicts or problems early if they are unable to reach a satisfactory resolution on their own

❏ Conduct periodic employee satisfaction surveys to keep your finger on "the pulse"

❏ Conduct regular training for employees and managers about how to deal with and resolve conflict

Where Do We Go from Here?

*❕*Like domestic violence, bullying behavior is always about power and control. It is perpetrated by individuals who lack normal inhibitions, devalue co-workers, and put their own need to control others above the employer's goals. The workplace bully destroys morale and employees' confidence; causes anxiety and depression; markedly lowers productivity; and impairs hiring and retention.[1]*❕*

It is axiomatic that unless and until a problem can be identified, actions cannot be taken to solve it, nor can strategies be developed by HR and their companies to minimize or prevent it. Hopefully, this book has been of assistance in helping you to better understand the phenomenon of workplace bullying — both what it is, and what it is not — and how to distinguish bullying from situations in which a manager is simply operating as a "tough boss."

As you can see by now, a bully-tolerant workplace can be quite pathological. A climate of fear can grip everyone — management included — making the decision-makers reluctant to hold the bully accountable for his or her mistreatment and abuse of employees. When individuals enter the workplace, they do not give up their right to be treated fairly and humanely in accordance with workplace norms for mutual respect. As noted by Harvey Hornstein:

> No matter what the circumstances, bosses may not abuse others. They may not lie, restrict, or dictate employees' behavior outside the workplace, threaten harm, or protect themselves at the expense of those more vulnerable. Positions of greater power in organizations' hierarchy do not grant license to show favoritism, humiliate or behave as masters or gods.[2]

All employers have the legal right to direct and control how work is done, and managers have a responsibility to direct and monitor workflow and give feedback (both positive and negative) about an employee's performance. Though tough bosses who set high performance standards may cause tension or stress among employees in a work situation, this is not workplace bullying.

Employees recognize the difference — which is distinct. The actions of "tough bosses" do not diminish an employee's feeling of self-worth and dignity, nor do their interactions with employees produce adverse personal or health effects. Simply stated and confirmed in the 2008 study discussed in Chapter 9, there is no *malice* in their workplace interactions with others. They act professionally and are focused on achieving high performance and positive results for the ultimate good of their organizations. Conversely, the behaviors of workplace bullies impact employees negatively, are intentionally done to cause harm or distress to their target, and suggest the presence of *malice* in most of what they do.

As with the issue of sexual harassment, it was only after the problem was more precisely defined and capable of being recognized that it was addressed — through employer policies, employee training, legislation, and enforcement. Until a specific law was passed to prohibit such conduct, many employers did not bother to take the steps to correct the problem. Workplace bullying may follow suit, though there is still much left to explore and learn about "this unpleasant form of workplace abuse which commonly masquerades as management."[3]

Fortunately, there appears to be a growing awareness and discussion about workplace bullying in the United States that has come about through the vigorous efforts of a number of American scholars and activists. In addition, the interest of unions, legal groups, and the media, as well as a number of books published on the topic in the popular media, have helped to shine a spotlight on this problem in recent years.

Given that we are entering into a time of deep and extreme skills shortages (for example, by 2010 there will reportedly be 10 million skilled-job vacancies),[4] it is more important than ever to ensure a climate of respect in order for employers to attract and retain key talent. In addition to being the right thing to do, there is also an element of self-preservation in the need to take preventive actions to stop bullying — even prior to a legislative mandate to do so.

As a result of the increasing attention to the phenomenon, perhaps the next decade will prove to be a more enlightened time for American organizations and the employees who work there. In the meantime, there is much work to be done to educate managers and their organizations about the importance of creating (and maintaining) a respectful workplace.

It is important that, as HR professionals, we collectively work to end workplace bullying. No person should have to experience the humiliating pain at work that was expressed by one of the participants in the study discussed in Chapter 9:

> I mean, that's where you just say that — literally — you wish
> the Earth would open up and suck you in. You know, like a
> big hole would just suck me in so I could get out of that.

Bullies poison their working environment by creating low morale, fear, anger, and depression among the targets and their co-workers, as well as their family and friends. Employers pay for this in lost efficiency, absenteeism, medical costs, high turnover, severance packages, and lawsuits.

It is my hope that you will agree that the business case made in this book for taking steps to eliminate bullying and for creating a "culture of respect" in your organization is compelling. The potential benefits include a more productive workplace, with better decision-making, reduced absenteeism and sick leave, lower medical costs, higher employee retention and satisfaction rates, and a reduced risk of legal action.

The negative impact of bullying is very real and entirely too high. Even one bully at work is too many. There is much work to be done — by both HR professionals and their management teams — to begin to build the kind of culture where professionalism and respect are the common, "normal" behaviors, and bullying is the ugly exception. Taking action to stop bullying in our organizations is important work. Let's all agree to get started — now.

Appendix: So Where Do *You* Stand on the Issue?

If you believe that legislation is necessary to stop bullying and get the attention of American organizations, there are a number of ways that you can get involved in the grassroots movement that is attempting to keep the "Healthy Workplace Bill" alive and under consideration throughout numerous states in the United States.

Some of the key resources that you can access for additional information and ways to get involved follow:

- Workplace Bullying Institute (www.bullyinginstitute.org). Education and research to stop bullying at work.
- Bully Busters (www.bullybusters.org). National coordinators of U.S. state legislative initiatives to stop workplace bullying.
- California Healthy Workplace Advocates (www.bullyfreeworkplace.org). The grassroots, Sacramento-based group of individuals committed to passing anti-bullying legislation in the country's largest state. The first bill was introduced in 2003. This group will not rest until there is a law with a record of faithful enforcement.
- Georgia Healthy Workplace Advocates (www.georgiahealthyworkplace advocates.com). To raise public awareness about workplace bullying and to compel lawmakers to prevent abusive environments through legislative reform.
- A Daily Dose of Happiness (www.thehappyguy.com/daily-happiness-free-ezine.html). Inspirational and positive messages that you can sign up to have delivered via email that can help targets look at life in a different way to get through the trauma of psychological violence in the workplace.
- Citizen Lobbying Guide (www.conservativeusa.org/lobbykit.htm). New York Healthy Workplace Act (NYHWA) sponsors have indicated that they will be creating a web page dedicated to the various ways individuals and groups across the state can get involved to promote the issue of psychological violence in the workplace and with the legislative effort as well. In the meantime, the Citizen Lobbying Guide is a good start to some of the activities NYHWA will be making available.

- Dr. Phil's Message Board on Workplace Bullying (www.drphil.com/messageboard/topic/283). Read about what others are going through in the workplace. This is an excellent website to understand the experience of a target of bullying and to find support from others who are going through a similar situation.

Endnotes

Chapter 1

[1] Hornstein (1996), p. 28.

[2] U.S. Workplace Bullying Survey (2007). This is the largest scientific survey of workplace bullying that has been conducted in the United States to-date. It was a poll conducted by Zogby International for the Workplace Bullying Institute in September 2007 and consisted of 7,740 online interviews with a representative sample of both full- and part-time workers across the United States. The survey is referred to throughout this book as the "U.S. Workplace Bullying Survey (2007)." Available: http://bullyinginstitute.org/zogby2007/WBIsurvey2007.pdf.

[3] Employment Law Alliance Survey (2007). Available: http://www.employmentlawalliance.com/en/node/2616.

[4] U.S. Workplace Bullying Survey (2007).

[5] Society for Human Resource Management and Ethics Resource Center Survey (2008). Available: http://www.ethics.org/ethics-today/0608/shrm-erc-survey.asp.

[6] U.S. Workplace Bullying Survey (2007).

[7] Hershcovis & Barling (2008).

[8] Id.

[9] Scripps Howard News Service (2007).

Chapter 2

[1] Federal Bureau of Investigation. [Online]. Available: http://www.fbi.gov/publications/violence.pdf.

[2] Hornstein (1996).

[3] Bing (1992).

[4] Marias & Herman (1997).

[5] Babiak & Hare (2006).

[6] Sutton (2007).

[7] Field (2004).

[8] Hornstein (1996).

[9] Mueller (2005).

[10] Namie & Namie (2003).

[11] Davenport, et al. (2005), p. 15.

[12] Sutton (2007).

[13] Hornstein (1996).

[14] Sutton (2007).

[15] Babiak & Hare (2006).

[16] Bing (1992).

[17] Namie & Namie (2003).

[18] Hornstein (1996).

[19] Lombardo & McCall (1984).

[20] Brodsky (1976).

[21] Namie & Namie (2003).
[22] Keashly (2001).
[23] Neuman (2004).
[24] Davenport, et al. (2005).
[25] Yamada (2000).
[26] Lutgen-Sandvik (2005).
[27] Tracy, Alberts, & Lutgen-Sandvik (2006).
[28] Workplace Bullying Institute website.
[29] U,S. Workplace Bullying Survey (2007).
[30] Hornstein (1996), p. 15-16.
[31] Workplace Bullying Institute 2008 Labor Day Survey.
[32] Einarsen, Raknes & Matthiesen (1994).
[33] Leymann (1996), p. 171.
[34] Davenport, Schwartz & Elliott (2005), p. 39.
[35] Workplace Bullying Institute website.
[36] Id.
[37] Id.

Chapter 3

[1] R. Wood, Director of the Colorado State Employee Assistance Program. [Online]. Available: http://www.colorado.gov/dpa/dhr/advisor/12-04adv.pdf.
[2] U.S. Workplace Bullying Survey (2007).
[3] Hornstein (1996), p. 50-60.
[4] Namie & Namie (2003).
[5] Egan, as outlined in Kelly (2005).
[6] Einarsen (1999).
[7] Yamada (2000), p. 477.
[8] Leymann (1996), p. 272.
[9] Randall (2001).
[10] Leymann (1996), p. 375.
[11] Workplace Bullying Institute 2008 Labor Day Survey.
[12] Id.

Chapter 4

[1] Toni Bowers, Head Blogs Editor at TechRepublic. [Online]. Available: http://blogs.techrepublic.com/careers/?p=3708&tag=nl.e101.
[2] My Bad Boss Contest (2007); Selvin (2007).
[3] Slonim (2007).
[4] American Psychological Association (April 2008).
[5] Employment Law Alliance Survey (2007).
[6] U.S. Workplace Bullying Survey (2007).
[7] Survey Report by the Society for Human Resource Management and the Ethics Resource Center (2008).
[8] U.S. Workplace Bullying Survey (2007).
[9] Workplace Bullying Institute website.
[10] Id.
[11] Id.

Chapter 5

[1] Anonymous participant interviewed for the research study of HR professionals discussed in Chapter 9.
[2] Yamada (2000).
[3] Brodsky (1976).
[4] Babiak & Hare (2006).
[5] Board & Fritzon (2005).
[6] Id. at pp. 17-32.
[7] Babiak & Hare (2006).

Chapter 6

[1] Pogo.
[2] Adams & Crawford (1992), p. 1.
[3] Hershcovis & Barling (2008).
[4] Tracy, Lutgen-Sandvik & Alberts (2006).
[5] Matthiesen & Einarsen (2004).
[6] Namie (2007), p. 47.
[7] Hoel & Cooper (2000).
[8] Vartia (1993).
[9] Leymann (1990).
[10] Bassman (1992).
[11] NIOSH Publication (1999).
[12] Sauter et al. (1990), as quoted in a report by the International Labour Organization of Geneva (see ILO report).
[13] Hoel, Sparks & Cooper (2001).
[14] American Institute of Stress (2007).
[15] Scripps Howard News Service (2007).
[16] Corporate Leavers Survey (2007).
[17] Annual Reports of Goldman Sachs, Google, Starbucks, and Amazon.com (2006).
[18] World Bank Statistics (Online).
[19] Gallup Organization Poll (2000).
[20] Buckingham, as quoted in Zipkin (2000), p. 1.
[21] U.S. Workplace Bullying Survey (2007).
[22] Id.
[23] Rayner (1999).
[24] Id.
[25] Id.
[26] Id.

Chapter 7

[1] Lewis Maltby, as quoted in Russell (2001), p. 4.
[2] Yamada (2000).
[3] Namie & Namie (2000); Cleveland & Kerst (1993).
[4] Namie (2007).
[5] U.S. Workplace Bullying Survey (2007).
[6] Title VII of the Civil Rights Act of 1964.
[7] See *Harris v. Forklift Systems, Inc.* and *Rogers v. EEOC*.
[8] U.S. Workplace Bullying Survey (2007).
[9] Americans with Disabilities Act of 1993.
[10] Stefan (1998).
[11] Age Discrimination in Employment Act of 1967.
[12] Occupational Safety and Health Act Fact Sheet on Workplace Violence, 2007.

[13] False Claims Act.
[14] *Torres v. Parkhouse Tire Service, Inc.*, 30 P.3d 57 (2001).
[15] *Raess v. Doescher*, No. 49S02-0710-CV-424 (Ind. Sup. Ct., April 8, 2008).
[16] McCord & Richardson (2001), p. 6.
[17] See *Hubbard v. United Press International*, 1983.
[18] *Shea v. Emmanuel College*, 425 Mass. 761 (1997).
[19] *Eserhut v. Heister*, 762 P.2d 6 (1988).
[20] Yamada (2005b), p. 12.
[21] Smith (2007).
[22] Id.
[23] Smith, R. (July 9, 2007).
[24] Oregon Department of Environmental Quality (2008).
[25] Id.
[26] Smith (2007).
[27] Id.
[28] Id.
[29] As reported at www.psuaaup.net/maraprilnewsletter.htm.
[30] Oregon Department of Environmental Quality (2008).
[31] Smith (2007).
[32] Labour Standards Act of Quebec, Canada (June 2004).
[33] Hankins (2007).
[34] This partnership consists of the European Trade Union Confederation, in collaboration with the Council of European Professional and Managerial Staff/ European Confederation of Executives and Managerial Staff Liaison Committee; Business Europe; the European Association of Craft, Small and Medium-Sized Enterprises; and the European Centre of Enterprises with Public Participation and of Enterprises of General Economic Interest.

Chapter 8

[1] Comments by Jo.
[2] Namie & Namie (2000); Field (1996).
[3] Healthy Workplace Bill. [Online]. Available: http://healthyworkplacebill.org/
[4] Yamada (2006).
[5] Healthy Workplace Bill.
[6] Yamada (2004), p. 476.
[7] Yamada (2007).
[8] Workplace Bullying Institute (2007).
[9] Bully-Free Workplace website (2008).
[10] Selvin (2007).
[11] Smith, R. (July 9, 2007).
[12] Id.
[13] Hyman (2008).
[14] Workplace Bullying Institute website (2008).
[15] Hyman (2008).
[16] Larson, M. (2008).

Chapter 9

[1] Comments by Maxine Weiss.
[2] Daniel, T.A. (2009).
[3] The author is grateful for the gift of time and insights offered by the study's participants, which included 20 HR practitioners, of which 15 (75 percent) were female and 5 (25 percent) were male. All of the participants were Caucasian. The mean age was 50.3

years and ranged from 32 to 65. The mean length of service with their organization was 19.9 years, and ranged from 3.5 to 40. The 20 participants were located in six different states in the Southeast region of the United States. Specifically, 5 were from West Virginia (25 percent); 9 were from Kentucky (45 percent); 1 was from Ohio (5 percent); 3 were from Florida (15 percent); 1 was from Pennsylvania (5 percent); and 1 was located in North Carolina (10 percent). The industries represented by these participants (with the number of HR practitioners involved in each specific industry noted in parentheses) were as follows: Non-profit (2); Consulting (4); Employment (2); Education (2); Services (1); Health Care (2); Diversified (4); Manufacturing (1); and Pharmaceuticals (2). Data about their marital or socioeconomic status, or their sexual orientation, was not collected.

[4] Andersson & Pearson (1999).
[5] Merriam-Webster Online Dictionary (2008).

Chapter 10

[1] Anonymous participant interviewed for the research study of HR professionals discussed in Chapter 9.
[2] 524 U.S. 775 (1998); see also 524 U.S. 742 (1998).
[3] Sarbanes-Oxley Act of 2002. [Online]. Available: www.sarbanes-oxley.com.
[4] See Lisa Guerin, *Essential Guide to Federal Employment Laws,* 2d edition (Nolo & SHRM, 2009), and Max Muller, *The Manager's Guide to HR* (AMACOM and SHRM, 2009).
[5] Sarbanes-Oxley Act of 2002.
[6] U.S. Workplace Bullying Survey (2007).
[7] Gary Namie, as quoted in Deschenaux, SHRM Online (2007).

Chapter 11

[1] Comment by Jo.
[2] Among others, these include: Horn, S. (2002). *Take the Bully by the Horns: Stop Unethical, Uncooperative, or Unpleasant People from Running and Ruining Your Life.* New York: St. Martin's Griffin; Namie, G. & Namie, R. (2003). *The Bully at Work: What You Can Do to Stop the Hurt and Reclaim Your Dignity on the Job.* Naperville, IL: Sourcebooks, Inc.; Mueller, R. (2005). *Bullying Bosses: A Survivor's Guide.* San Francisco: Bullying Bosses.com; Futterman, S. (2004). *When You Work for a Bully: Assessing Your Options and Taking Action.* Montvale, NJ: Croce Publishing Group; and Kohut, M.R. (2008). *The Complete Guide to Understanding, Controlling and Stopping Bullies & Bullying at Work.* Ocala, FL: Atlantic Publishing Group.
[3] Horn, S. (2002).
[4] "What Bullied Targets Can Do," Workplace Bullying Institute. [Online] Available at http://www.bullyinginstitute.org/education/bbstudies/3step.html.
[5] Namie, G. & Namie, R. (2003), pp. 225-66.
[6] Hornstein, H. (1996). *Brutal Bosses and their Prey: How to Identify and Overcome Abuse in the Workplace.* New York: Riverhead Books, pp. 83-100.
[7] Davenport, N., Distler Schwartz, R. & Pursell Elliott, G. (1999, reprinted 2005). *Mobbing: Emotional Abuse in the American Workplace.* Ames, IA: Civil Society Publishing.
[8] Namie, G. & Namie, R. (2003). *The Bully at Work.* Naperville, IL: Sourcebooks, Inc., pp. 116-28.
[9] Davenport, et al. (1999), pp. 121-9.
[10] Id. at pp. 131-207.
[11] Futterman, S. (2004), p. 32.
[12] U.S. Workplace Bullying Survey (2007).

[13] Hornstein (1996), pp. 121-6.
[14] U.S. Workplace Bullying Survey (2007).
[15] Salin, D. (2008).
[16] Id. at p. 247.
[17] Salin, D. (2008).
[18] Smith, R. (July 9, 2007).
[19] Id.
[20] Richards & Daly (2003), p. 257.
[21] U.S. Workplace Bullying Survey (2007).
[22] Davenport, et al. (1999), pp. 141-5.
[23] Futterman, S. (2004), p. 196.
[24] U.S. Workplace Bullying Survey (2007).
[25] Id.
[26] Salin, D. (2008).
[27] Id.
[28] U.S. Workplace Bullying Survey (2007).
[29] Id.
[30] Id.
[31] Namie, G. & Namie, R. (2003). *The Bully at Work*. Naperville, IL: Sourcebooks, Inc.

Chapter 12

[1] Tim Field (Online).
[2] "Workplace Bullying Policy" available at www.shrm.org/TemplatesTools/Samples/Policies/Pages/CMS_018350.aspx.
[3] "Investigating Workplace Conduct" available at www.shrm.org/TemplatesTools/Samples/Policies/Pages/CMS_000550.aspx.
[4] "Sexual and Other Unlawful Harassment" available at www.shrm.org/TemplatesTools/Samples/Policies/Pages/CMS_007624.aspx.

Chapter 13

[1] Wood, R. (2004).
[2] Hornstein (1996), p. 143.
[3] Field (1996), p. xxii.
[4] Larson (2008).

References

Adams, A. (1992). *Bullying at work: How to confront and overcome it.* London: Virago Press.

Adams, A. & Crawford, N. (1992). *Bullying at work.* London: Virago Press.

Age Discrimination in Employment Act of 1967. [Online]. Available: www.eeoc.gov/policy/adea.html.

American Bar Association (May 22, 2007). "Buried bodies, bad apples and law firm bullies: Lawyer ethics conference deals with tough issues." [Online]. Available: www.abanews.org.

American Institute of Stress (2007). [Online]. Available: www.stress.org/job.htm.

Americans with Disabilities Act (1993). [Online]. Available: www.doj.gov/crt/ada/adahom1.htm.

American Psychological Association (March 9, 2008). "Bullying More Harmful than Sexual Harassment on the Job, Say Researchers." *Science Daily.* [Online]. Available: www.sciencedaily.com/releases/2008/03/080308090927.htm.

American Psychological Association (April 2008). *Monitor on Psychology, 39* (4). [Online]. Available: www.apa.org/monitor/2008/04/workplace_awards.html.

Andersson, L.M. & Pearson, C.M. (1999). "Tit for tat? The spiralling effect of incivility in the workplace." *Academy of Management Review, 24,* 452-71.

Annual Reports of Goldman Sachs, Google, Starbucks, and Amazon. com for the year ending 2006. [Online]. Available: www.goldmansachs.com, www.investor.google.com, http://library.corporate-ir.net, http://media. corporate-ir.net.

Babiak, P. & Hare, R.D. (2006). *Snakes in suits.* New York: Harper Collins.

Bassman, E.S. (1992). *Abuse in the workplace: Management remedies and bottom line impact.* Westport, CT: Quorum Books.

Bing, S. (1992). *Crazy bosses: spotting them, serving them, surviving them.* New York: William Morrow.

Board, B.J. & Fritzon, K.F. (2005). "Disordered personalities at work." *Psychology, Crime and Law, 11,* 17-32.

Brodsky, C.M. (1976). *The harassed worker.* Toronto, ON: Lexington Books.

Bully-Free Workplace website (2008). [Online]. Available: www. bullyfreeworkplace.org.

Bully Busters website (2008). [Online]. Available: www.bullybusters. org.

Civil Rights Act of 1964. [Online]. Available: http://usinfo.state. gov/usa/infousa/laws/majorlawscivilr19.htm.

Cleveland, J.N. & Kerst, M.E. (1993). "Sexual harassment and perceptions of power: An under-articulated relationship." *Journal of Vocational Behavior, 42*(1), 49-67.

Corporate Leavers Survey (2007). [Online]. Available: www.lpfi. org/workplace/corporateleavers.html.

Cranshaw, L. (2005). *Coaching Abrasive Executives: Exploring the Use of Empathy in Constructing Less Destructive Interpersonal Management Strategies.* Fielding Graduate University Doctoral Dissertation.

Daniel, T.A. (2009). *"Tough Boss" or Workplace Bully: A Grounded Theory Study of Insights from Human Resource Professionals.* Doctoral Dissertation, Fielding Graduate University.

Davenport, N., Schwartz, R. & Elliot, G. (2005). *Mobbing: emotional abuse in the American workplace.* Ames, IA: Civil Society Publishing.

Deschenaux, J. (2007). "Experts: Anti-Bullying Policies Increase Productivity, Add to Bottom Line," SHRM Workplace Law Library - Employee Relations. [Online]. Available: www.shrm.org/LegalIssues/ EmploymentLawAreas/Pages/CMS_023079.aspx.

Einarsen, S., Raknes, B.I., Matthiesen, S.B. & Hellesoy, O.H. (1994). *Bullying and severe interpersonal conflicts: Unhealthy interaction at work*. Sureid grend. Sigma Forlag.

Einarsen, S. (1999). "The nature and causes of bullying at work." *International Journal of Manpower, 20*(1/2), 16-27.

Employment Law Alliance Survey (2007). [Online]. Available: www. employmentlawalliance.com.

Eserhut v. Heister, 762 P.2d 6 (1988).

False Claims Act, Title 31, Chapter 37, Section 3729 of the U.S. Code. [Online]. Available: http://www.cms.hhs.gov/smdl/downloads/SMD032207Att2.pdf.

Federal Bureau of Investigation. [Online]. Available: www.fbi.gov/publications/violence.pdf.

Field, T. (1996). *Bully in sight*. Wantage, Oxfordshire: Wessex Press.

Field, T. (2004). [Online]. Available: www.bullyoffline.org/workbully/quotes.htm.

Futterman, S. (2004). *When you work for a bully: Assessing your options and taking action*. Montvale, NJ: Croce Publishing Group Gallup Organizational Poll (2000). [Online]. Available: www.pdkintl.org/kappan/kpol0009.htm.

Gallup Organizational Poll (2000). [Online]. Available: www.pdkintl. org/kappan/kpol0009.htm.

Hankins, R. (September 1, 2007). "States consider legislation to cut office bullies down to size." *Workplace Horizons*. [Online]. Available: www. workplacehorizons.com.

Harris v. Forklift Systems, Inc., 510 U.S. 17 (1993) at p. 22.

Healthy Workplace Bill. [Online]. Available: http://healthyworkplacebill.org/.

Hershcovis, M.S. & Barling, J. (2008). "Outcomes of workplace aggression and sexual harassment: A meta-analytic comparison." Presented at the 7th Annual Work, Stress, & Health Conference, Washington, DC.

Hoel, H. & Cooper, C.L. (2000). "Destructive conflict and bullying at work." Manchester School of Management, University of Manchester Institute of Science and Technology.

Hoel, H., Sparks, K. & Cooper, C. (2001). "Origins of bullying: Theoretical frameworks for exploring bullying." In N. Tehrani (ed.) Building a culture of respect: Managing bullying at work (pp. 3-19). London: Taylor & Francis.

Horn, S. (2002). *Take the bully by the horns: Stop unethical, uncooperative, or unpleasant people from running and ruining your life.* New York: St. Martin's Griffin.

Hornstein, H.A. (1996). *Brutal bosses and their prey: how to identify and overcome abuse in the workplace.* New York: Riverhead Books.

Hubbard v. United Press International, Inc., 330 N.W.2d 428, 429 (Minn. 1983).

Hyman, J. [Online]. Available: http://ohioemploymentlaw.blogspot.com/2008/08/anti-bullying-policies.html.

International Labour Report of Geneva. [Online]. Available: http://oldweb.unicz.it/lavoro/ILOCOST.pdf.

Jo, as cited online at http://althouse.blogspot.com/2007/08/half-of-working-americans-49-have.html.

Kelly, D.J. (2005). "Reviewing workplace bullying: strengthening approaches to a complex phenomenon." *Journal of Occupational Health and Safety - Australia and New Zealand*, 21(6), 551-64.

Kohut, M.R. (2008). *The Complete Guide to Understanding, Controlling and Stopping Bullies & Bullying at Work.* Ocala, FL: Atlantic Publishing Group.

Larson, M. (2008). [Online]. Available: www.workforce.com/section/09/feature/25/00/19/ndex.html.

Leymann, H. (1990). "Moral harassment and psychological terror at workplaces." *Violence and Victims*, 5(2), 119-26.

Leymann, H. (1996). "The content and development of mobbing at work." *European Journal of Work & Organizational Psychology*, 5(2), 165-84.

Lombardo, M.M., & McCall, M.W., Jr. (January 1984). The intolerable boss. *Psychology Today*, 45–48.

Malice. (2008). In Merriam-Webster Online Dictionary. Retrieved August 16, 2008, from www.merriam-webster.com/dictionary/malice.

Marias, M. & Herman, S. (1997). *Corporate Hyenas at Work.* Johannesburg: Kagiso Publishers.

Matthiesen, S.B. & Einarsen, S. (2004). "Psychiatric distress and symptoms of PTSD among victims of bullying at work." *British Journal of Guidance and Counselling*, 32, 335-56.

Maxine Weiss, as reported online at http://althouse.blogspot.com/2007/08/half-of-working-americans-49-have.html.

McCord, L.B. & Richardson, J.B. (Fall 2001). "Are workplace bullies sabotaging your ability to compete?" *Graziadio Business Report*, Pepperdine University.

Mueller, R. (2005). *Bullying bosses: A survivor's guide*. San Francisco: BullyingBosses.com.

My Bad Boss Contest (2007). [Online]. Available: www. workingamerica.org/badboss/sutton.cfm.

Namie, G. & Namie, R. (2000). "Workplace bullying: The silent epidemic." *Employee Rights Quarterly, 1* (2), 1-12.

Namie, G. & Namie, R. (2003). *The bully at work: What you can do to stop the hurt and reclaim your dignity on the job*. Naperville, IL: Sourcebooks.

Namie, G. (2007). "The challenge of workplace bullying." *Employment Relations Today, 34*(2, Summer 2007), 43-51.

National Institute for Occupational Safety and Health, Stress at Work Publication (1999). No. 99-101. [Online]. Available: www.cdc.gov/ niosh/topics/stress/.

Neuman, J.H. (2004). The role of the workplace in workplace bullying. *Perspectives on Work*, 40, 7-32.

Occupational Health and Safety Act Fact Sheet on Workplace Violence. [Online]. Available: www.osha.gov/OshDoc/data_General_Facts/ factsheet-workplace-violence.pdf.

Yamada, D.C. (2006). "The 'Healthy Workplace' Bill: A Model Act." [Online]. Available: www.bullyinginstitute.org.

Yamada, D.C. (June 2007). "Potential legal protections and liabilities for workplace bullying." [Online]. Available: www.newworkplaceinstitute. org.

Zipkin, A. (June 26, 2000). "Kinder, gentler workplace replaces era of tough boss." *The Oklahoma City Journal Record*.

Useful Websites

Bad Bossology (www.badbossology.com/strategies)
Bully Busters (www.bullybusters.org)
Bullying and Emotional Intelligence (www.bullyeq.com)
Bully Online (www.bullyonline.org)
Bully Offline (www.bullyoffline.org)
eBoss Watch (www.ebosswatch.com)
Monster.com Forum (content.monster.com/articles/3493/18150/1/default.aspx)
New Workplace Institute (www.newworkplaceinstitute.org)
New York Healthy Workplace Advocates (www.nyhwa.org/)
Project for Wellness and Work-life (www.asu.edu/clas/communication/about/wellness/)
The Work Doctor (www.workdoctor.com)
Wikipedia on Workplace Bullying (www.wikipedia.org/wiki/workplace_bullying)
Workplace Bullying Institute (www.bullyinginstitute.org)
Workbully Support Group (health.groups.yahoo.com/group/workbully-suppport/links)

Index

Acknowledgments

This book would not have been written without the participation of the HR practitioners who agreed to be interviewed for my research. They enthusiastically offered their time and shared insights about their personal experiences with bullying, as well as their observations about bullying directed toward others at work. Their motive was selfless — an effort to assist in the identification and clarification about what workplace bullying is (and is not) for the benefit of the profession.

Gary Namie, Ph.D.—activist, scholar, and director of the Workplace Bullying Institute — provided an unexpected gift as a result of his gracious advance review of the book. His comments and suggestions ensured that the content of the book is as technically accurate and up-to-date as possible.

Many thanks also go to Margaret A. Evans, Ph.D., SPHR, who is the Director of Human Resources at the Government Employees Health Association, Inc. and Mark A. Lies II of Seyfarth Shaw LLP for their help in reviewing the manuscript and making very helpful suggestions.

This book was also significantly strengthened by the support of my best friend, colleague, and husband, Gary S. Metcalf, Ph.D. — a gifted scholar and mind-expanding teacher with a unique gift of seeing what everyone else has seen in new ways. Gary spent countless hours discussing many new and complex ideas with me, all of which were essential to the development and refinement of the book's content and conceptual framework.

About the Author

Teresa A. Daniel, J.D., Ph.D. — Employment Lawyer, HR Consultant, MBA Faculty, and Author — is the President & Owner of InsideOut HR Solutions PLLC located in Ashland, Kentucky (www.insideout.bz). Established in 1998, the firm provides HR-related counsel and proactive training solutions to both corporations and small businesses. Teri also provides keynote speeches and hands-on workshops about workplace bullying, sexual harassment, and other people-related legal issues.

Teri is an Associate Graduate Faculty member in both the executive and traditional MBA Programs at Marshall University, where she teaches Leadership Ethics and Business Law. She also teaches online courses for Kaplan University in Business Law and Ethics. Prior to joining the academic world, she spent more than 15 years working for a *Fortune* 50 company in the areas of employment law and human resources.

She was named a Fulbright Senior Scholar in 2004 and was honored in 2002 as a Distinguished Alumnus at Centre College in Danville, Kentucky. She is the author of two other HR-related books, *The Management of People in Mergers & Acquisitions* and *Cash Balance Pension Plans: A Practical Primer*, and numerous SHRM white papers.

She can be reached via e-mail at: TeresaAnnDaniel@gmail.com.